HOW TO TRAIN YOUR THINKING

SHARPEN YOUR MIND TO THINK BIGGER AND
MATERIALIZE YOUR DREAMS

D1739301

WISDOM UNIVERSITY

I

Free Bonus #2

Thinking Guide Flex Your Wisdom Muscle

FLEX YOUR WISDOM MUSCLE

37 Enlightening Quotes From
The Greatest Minds Of All Time
To Sharpen Your Thinking

WISDOM UNIVERSITY

A glimpse into what you'll discover inside:

✓ How to expose the sneaky flaws in your thinking and what it takes to fix them (the included solutions are dead-simple)

✓ Dozens of foolproof strategies to make sound and regret-free decisions leading you to a life of certainty and fulfillment

✓ How to elevate your rationality to extraordinary levels (this will put you on a level with Bill Gates, Elon Musk and Warren Buffett)

✓ Hidden gems of wisdom to guide your thoughts and actions (gathered from the smartest minds of all time)

Free Bonus #3

Get All Our Upcoming Books FOR FREE (Yes, you've read that right!)

Get exclusive access to our books before they hit the online shelves and enjoy them for free.

Take me to wisdom-university.net for my free bonuses!

(Or simply scan the code with your camera)

Scan Me

INTRODUCTION

What if I told you that the phrase wasn't "More money: More problems" but actually "More problems: More money"?

The initial phrase, "More money: more problems," suggests that success/money/power is the source of many a problem and that the more of it you attain, the more problems will arise from it. To some extent, there is some truth to the phrase because there is undoubtedly a relationship between the two concepts.

The issues of wealthy people are indeed different from those of the average Joe, but that doesn't mean their problems are more numerous or significant than those with fewer resources. For example, a wealthy person may dine exotically every night, while the average person may eat a casserole.

The denominating factor here is hunger. How an individual addresses the problem depends on them and the resources in their possession. For some reason, it's difficult to imagine the wealthy on the side of the highway changing a flat tire or even waiting for Triple-A. Whereas, the regular person may have changed a tire twice this month already.

Is hunger a "bigger problem" for the average person? Hunger is an issue for every person, and although the way one can address the issue, it affects everyone the same. The "problem" isn't hunger itself, but the capacity to address and hopefully rectify the issue.

In search of companionship, the wealthy person and the regular just the same may still have great difficulty finding the appropriate companion. The wealthy person struggles to find someone that appreciates the kind of person he is and not how much he is worth. The regular person struggles to find someone willing to work together to achieve success. The struggle is real in both instances.

When one thinks of successful people—names such as Bill Gates, Elon Musk, Jeff Bezos, and Warren Buffet—careful examination will reveal an underlying trend amongst them and other successful individuals, and it's not as simple as more money: more problems. It is quite the opposite.

Most of these success stories are based on the individual addressing and solving an important issue that as a result benefited them greatly financially. Bill Gates addressed the issue of worldwide connectivity and communication making it easier and faster. Elon Musk addresses the issue of energy consumption and provides alternatives to mainstream options for cars and electronics. Jeff Bezos made the online shopping experience more enjoyable while Warren Buffet made investing simpler by handling all the guesswork and improving portfolios.

Problems can be opportunities in disguise. They are a chance to test ourselves and gain useful knowledge and experience. The difference between successful people and the not-so-successful is that the latter fails to recognize their problems are opportunities. Instead, they may even avoid them to maintain their peace of mind.

Successful people see problems as the potential opportunities that they are. Moreover, they have a desired outcome in mind, and therefore, their actions will be guided by their ability and motivation to address the problem. This subtle difference in awareness makes all the difference. One cannot make use of an opportunity if it is not recognized as such.

The success-problem relationship can also be applied to the mind and performance. When individuals experience difficulty with thought, frustration and anxiety are likely to be present; however, these are the times with the greatest potential for growth and success.

Difficult, challenging thoughts are the exact instances where thinking can be improved. At the very least, these opportunities give individuals the chance to test their mettle, validate their efforts and provide useful feedback. Similar to how successful people use problems to their benefit, so too must individuals use the mental obstacle course that is life to improve thinking.

Do you think Warren Buffet wakes up in the middle night in his million-dollar home with the woes of other people's money on their behalf? Or that Bill Gates falls into depression knowing that he helped to connect the world and improve communication? Maybe you'll believe that Elon Musk is saddened by the frantic state of the fuel industry.

Using problematic situations to one's benefit has been going on for ages and is more common than one may realize. For centuries, nations and groups have been profiting from war. More war means more weapons to be created, which means more money for weapons manufacturers. Sickness and disease are the money cow of the pharmaceutical industry while there are churches filled with lost and misguided souls with full bank accounts.

Would it not be wise to also follow suit—not generate further destruction but—in using problems to your benefit? Whether physical, mental, emotional, or spiritual, problems and dilemmas are the cornerstone for improvement, as paradoxical as it may seem.

This book is intended to provide insight into and guidance for the development of thought. The first three chapters lay the foundation for understanding the nature of one's thought and highlight the connection between thought and action. The next three chapters draw attention to important controllable external and internal factors that affect thought. The latter chapters discuss how to apply this newfound understanding to one's benefit–how to think bigger.

Wanting improvement is equivalent to wanting change. Coming from the island nation of Dominica, my curious nature and thirst for knowledge eventually caused me to travel and gain valuable life experience. After living, studying, and eventually working in Asia for more than a decade, I am multilingual and have experience teaching different ages, backgrounds, cultures, and circumstances. One cannot improve and yet remain the same.

If you are ready and willing to change, then let us begin the transformation.

Kevaughn Francis

YOU AND YOUR THINKING

Nature & Nurture

Enrico Fermi, Wolfgang Amadeus Mozart, Blaise Pascal, and Clara Schumann: What do they share in common? At first glance, we may recognize these names for their popularity given their respective contributions to the world. However, another common denominator among the aforementioned is that they were all child prodigies. From a very young age, they began to display behaviors and attitudes incomparable to those of higher age and wider experience.

If we further examine child prodigies, we will notice that their method of thinking and approach to problem-solving is markedly different, or at the very least efficaciously superior, to those of their respective times. Moreover, there is significant research on our inefficacies as thinkers and the resulting sub-optimal or even negative consequences [123]. Therefore it comes as no surprise that improved thinking skills will yield more favorable results and improve the overall efficacy of the thinking process, accomplishing more in less time.

According to psychologist Joanne Ruthsatz, "I would say for a true prodigy it's as rare as 1 in 5 million or 1 in 10 million"[4]. Thinking is a skill, and unless you are part of that small naturally gifted percentile, a structured approach is the best way to improve your thinking skills. There are numerous resources and applicable strategies available for improving thinking. An often overlooked concept, yet central to this book, is metacognition: understanding how and why you think the way you do.

There is no denying the innate nature of intelligence and ability. Some people are just born talented, or more specifically, with a greater capacity for thought and problem-solving. Deep down, all parents believe that their child is a genius, or at least capable of genius contributions, and rightfully so. However, genetics is not the only path to improved thinking.

The nurture side of the argument suggests that the environment and circumstances surrounding the individual play significant roles in the formation of thought and associated thinking strategies. The way that someone perceives and interacts with the world around them (past, present, or future) shapes their mind and beliefs greatly.

Let's consider two individuals, A and B, faced with the same problem: a broken computer. A comes from a wealthy background and is accustomed to being provided for or having financial means. Whereas B comes from a financially unstable background and, as a result, constantly faces some form of hardship.

The thought process of A will veer towards replacing the laptop entirely. Given their circumstances, replacing the computer would be the best course of action. However, B would be almost compelled to follow a different trend of thought given their less-than-ideal circumstances. Repair would more likely be the first option to address the issue.

Your environment solely doesn't dictate your thought processes, so there is no guarantee that people with similar backgrounds to A and B would approach that situation. You can truly maximize your thinking potential by addressing factors within your control, specifically from the nurture aspect.

To be able to use anything to its maximum potential, one must first understand how it works. The best source of insight into your way of thinking is through the process of metacognition.

Thinking About Thinking

Metacognition refers to the awareness and understanding of one's thought processes. People naturally acquire and refine their metacognitive skills through experience and with practice. Thus more experienced or older learners would make better use of them than less experienced or younger ones.

For instance, the way two persons approach completing a thousand-piece puzzle may differ significantly. While the less experienced individual debates where to start— edge or center—the more experienced person focuses on organizing the puzzle pieces by color and number of edges before beginning. As a result of this subtle application of cognitive skills, experience completes the puzzle in 20 minutes while inexperience takes two hours.

Flavell proposed four components of metacognition including metacognitive knowledge, metacognitive experiences, skills (strategies), and goals (tasks). The quality of and relationship between these components guide the thinking process and inevitably dictate the resulting actions [5].

For instance, a student may believe themselves to be better at mathematics than science (knowledge), perhaps due to their perceived difficulty of science (experience). Therefore they decide to allocate more time to studying science (strategy) to improve their grades (goal).

Metacognitive knowledge refers to what people know about their cognitive abilities as well as those of others. It mainly concerns how the individual goes about problem-solving. Metacognitive knowledge is continuously enriched, updated, and differentiated by integrating information from the conscious monitoring of cognition, through observation of one's and others' behavior and their outcomes when dealing with specific tasks in various contexts [6].

Metacognitive experiences are essentially the thoughts and feelings associated with undertaking a task or processing its relevant information. They provide useful feedback that makes the person aware of the state of their cognition and triggers control processes of self-regulation [7].

For example, a student who has been failing Algebra all semester will react differently from a top student to the news of a pop quiz. This difference in reaction is not necessarily due to the lack of knowledge of the failing student, but more based on their previous difficulties with the subject.

These experiences take the form of metacognitive feelings, metacognitive judgments, and task-specific knowledge [8]. Feelings of knowing, familiarity, and confidence are some indicative metacognitive feelings extensively studied in metamemory research [9].

Metacognitive skills refer to the deliberate use of strategies to control cognition [10]. The emphasis is on the intentional use of these skills in achieving a goal. Much like the actions of blinking and winking that involve similar processes, the latter is a deliberate and controlled action while the previous has more of an automatic (unconscious) nature.

In addition, the desired goal of each action is completely different. Blinking is done for the purpose of hydrating the surface of the eyeballs whereas winking can be understood as a flirtatious gesture.

Metacognitive skills comprise various strategies for orientation, planning, regulation of cognitive processing, monitoring the execution of planned action, and strategies for the evaluation of the outcome of task processing [11].

For example, an experienced mechanic would possess great skill in diagnosing, repairing, and maintaining a vehicle. The greater the experience, the greater the confidence and associated skill.

For instance, in order to repair a broken down car (goal), the mechanic will first have to diagnose the problem and then choose the most suitable method for repair (strategy and planning). The method of repair can depend on many factors including the availability of parts, time, budget of the customer, etc.

After attempting to repair the vehicle, the mechanic will now ensure that the repair is operating as it should. Not only the repair itself, but the entire system is monitored as it relates to the newly repaired part(s) and its function within the vehicle system (monitoring).

If the problem was rectified, then the entire car system would return to regular functioning. Depending on the circumstance, the newly repaired part could even improve performance on a whole. Conversely, after an attempt to repair, the problem could remain or cause other parts of the system to malfunction (evaluation).

If the repair was unsuccessful, then an experienced mechanic would reevaluate his approach. Possibly he could alter his strategy for repair or reassess the possible sources of the problem. A less skilled mechanic may simply repeat the failed attempt more carefully or blame the failure on a lack of resources.

For metacognitive skills to be activated, there needs to be an awareness of one's fluency in cognitive processing. The latter information is conveyed by metacognitive experiences, such as feelings of familiarity, difficulty, or of confidence. Thus, metacognitive experience provides the input that triggers metacognitive skills, either directly or indirectly, through metacognitive knowledge.

In the earlier example with the pop quiz, the metacognitive experience of the top-performing student would likely involve feelings of familiarity and confidence derived from their past successes associated with the topic. As a result, minimal regulation is required. They feel prepared.

The unprepared student, on the other hand, would be greeted by feelings of anxiety and difficulty deriving from their past failures associated with the topic. They are aware of their inadequacies and their likely results but have no apparent way to regulate their thought processing.

Until you find out more about the advantages and limitations of your particular way of thinking, you will find great difficulty altering and developing your mental capabilities.

Looking Under The Hood

Allan F. Mogensen is often quoted for his saying, "work smarter, not harder," but how does one go about achieving that? Level and quality of education are important indicators of mental capacity and aptitude. However, results from one study by Perkins supported the conclusion that education has a significant but very small effect on informal reasoning (the ability to validate or falsify a claim) [12]. That is to say, an individual with an Ivy League education doesn't equate to a big thinker.

There is no universal answer to expanding your thinking but rather a set of guiding principles and vital areas of development that must be addressed respectively to the individual circumstance. One person's area of focus may be different from another, yet the same guiding principles may be applied to both. Before you can work smarter, you need to think smarter.

Research has shown that metacognitive training, even if administered for a short time, can improve performance considerably [13]. However, cognitive skills are not taught in the traditional education system, and as a result, our metacognitive abilities are heavily based on our life experiences: trial and error. The responsibility lies on each individual to address the weaknesses of their metacognitive abilities through whatever means are available.

When experience is supplemented with sound cognitive strategies, a strong foundation for success is set even before any action is taken. Studies have shown that the relationship between self-efficacy and performance is partially mediated by metacognition [14]. Additional research exists linking improved metacognitive skills to mathematical performance, problem-solving, reading, and comprehension [15]. Our thinking is the basis for how we perceive and live our lives.

Gaining insight into the way you think leads to a better understanding of yourself, your actions, and your decisions. Therefore, you can better position yourself to obtain the desired outcome. If you struggle with alcoholism, watching the game with friends at a bar would not be the best idea. If you are on a diet, you would not have dinner at an all-you-can-eat restaurant. This cognizant approach to life and decision-making will undoubtedly affect your trajectory in life.

The journey to thinking bigger begins with assessing and analyzing one's knowledge, experiences, cognitive skills, and circumstances. It's safe to say that although we could use a pocket map to get around, we can all appreciate the benefits of using a GPS instead.

The mind is like any piece of machinery. Looking under the hood would provide valuable insight into its operation, maintenance, and repair. Take a car, for example. Before you purchase a vehicle, many questions need to be asked concerning its function, capabilities, and cost. From this acquired knowledge, you can determine if that vehicle is best suited to your needs.

Conversely, individuals without this valuable knowledge about the vehicle would make their decision based on superficial factors, like color and popularity, or the opinion of others. Consequently, the vehicle purchased, although it could still be used for transportation, was not the most suitable option. As a result, you face unforeseen problems like gas usage, 4WD capability, or even trunk space.

Understanding the desired result of your thought process and making sure you have the knowledge and metacognitive skills to achieve said result are crucial steps to applying your thought process more universally.

Action Steps

Knowledge is power, and in this case, knowledge of your metacognitive abilities is of tremendous value. Some of the most useful information you can obtain is from self-observation. You are the expert on all things concerning you including the way you think.

We cannot overstate the value of one's environment and circumstances in the formation and development of metacognition, but they are variables whose effects cannot always be predicted. As a result, it is better to focus on the impact of these variables on the acquisition and development of our metacognitive skills and tendencies.

Taking into consideration observatory skills and environmental factors, here are some useful hints for improving your metacognition:

1. Do self-questioning: Scrutiny of one's feelings, actions, and motivations (e.g., "What do I already know about this topic? How have I solved problems like this before?"). Self-questioning establishes a starting point or base of knowledge on the topic. It brings into view the cognitive status quo, tells us if we need to do more research before we begin, or if a different approach could have better results than a previous one.

2. Learn to be flexible: Flexibility is always a good thing, and not just the yoga kind. The flexibility of the mind allows you to adapt to certain situations especially when things do not go as planned. It is something that has to be learned with experience. Actively and consciously look at difficult circumstances as opportunities to develop flexibility of the mind and not only as troublesome occurrences.

3. Practice preparation: Have you ever been halfway through preparing a meal and realized that you are missing a couple of key ingredients? Unfortunately, our options and choices are limited at that time, and we are left with a less desirable result. Preparation is key. Make preparation a vital part of any process or action. If you are going to cook, don't just decide on a meal and then begin. Take stock of the food and kitchen utensils before you start cooking anything. By doing this, we know exactly what ingredients are available and what meal can be cooked with them.

4. Avoid comfort zones: Live in a nomadic mental space. Never get too comfortable in one area of expertise or too

focused on certain outcomes. By living outside our comfort zones, we force our minds to always be in a more receptive state by taking in new information and attempting new strategies to deal with unfamiliar situations.

5. Do your own research: With enough pertinent information on a topic, especially concerning your metacognition, one can start to bury ineffective strategies that were previously used and discover newer and more applicable strategies to the thinking process.

Even if you have been using a typewriter your entire life and your skills with it are impeccable, it cannot compare with the sheer capabilities of a laptop computer to not only type but research and store information. With that in mind, it's time to get out that shovel and bury that ancient tool.

6. Think critically: The cultivation of critical reasoning ability has been an objective of teachers of philosophy, logic, and rhetoric, among other subjects, for a very long time. It is easy to get swayed by the opinion and results of others, but critical thinking allows us to form an objective opinion and as a result, apply the best course of action for the desired outcome.

Just because something worked for someone, it doesn't mean it will work for you. It is all right to swim against the tide sometimes, especially if your course was determined critically and not on a whim or emotional inclination. Some of the greatest discoveries and breakthroughs were made by those who dared to swim against the tides.

7. Learn more skills: Although we may not realize the value of learning new and different skills, many of the strategies used when dealing with one situation are transferrable to other seemingly less similar situations. For example, strategies and skills learned from playing video games, like eye-hand coordination, could be useful for sports like tennis, ping-pong, or even pool.

As Sun Tzu observed, "Strategy without tactics is the slowest route to victory. Tactics without strategy is the noise before defeat." The first and most crucial step in any endeavor is preparation. Preparing your mind and equipping it with the necessary tools serve as the first step in changing the way you think.

Key Reader Takeaways

- Thinking is an improvable skill.
- Learning about metacognition, particularly your own, is central to improving thinking.
- We think based on what we know and understand.
- Thinking skills are not always taught. Each individual has the responsibility of developing their thinking habits.
- Observation of self and surroundings is the foundation for understanding your thinking.

2

THE PRINCIPLE OF CONTROLLED ACTION

Hero Mode Activated

One day while taking a leisurely walk, you notice some smoke rising from a building in the distance. You walk over there in hopes of satisfying your curiosity and discover that the local bakery had caught fire.

A crowd of onlookers begins to gather as they wait for the fire department to arrive. It's safe to say that no one would be entering that building in an attempt to save the chocolate-stuffed croissants or their son Billy's birthday cake.

The only desired outcome in that situation would be to extinguish the fire, which will be handled by the professionals already en route. Bystanders feel no need to act or get involved apart from their detailed filmography and online dissemination of current events. You look on in awe and hope that the situation can be resolved quickly.

On the other hand, if it were discovered that there were people still trapped in that burning building, then that would be an entirely different scenario. Many bystanders would be more obliged to act since they now possess another desired outcome in the safe rescue of the aforementioned trapped individuals.

Rescue falls under the domain of the firefighters, therefore, not everyone would feel the need to get involved. Some, however, may feel immediate action is necessary since the firefighters may not make it in time. Although the rescue is a shared goal among the firefighters and bystanders, only some bystanders take subsequent action. You commend them on their bravery and continue to look on in anticipation of the result.

Suddenly, someone identifies the persons trapped in the building to be your wife and child. At that moment, there would be no one with a greater desire to achieve the safe rescue of your family than yourself. A swell of desire erupts so powerfully that you are already halfway up the burning building before you can finish your thought.

There appears to be general agreement among social psychologists that most human behavior is goal-oriented [1]. Therefore, the difference between action and inaction is the presence, or lack thereof, of a goal or desired outcome. Furthermore, the extent of desire to attain said goals will determine the degree to which effort is applied.

Intentions

Actions are controlled by intention, but not all intentions are carried out; some are abandoned altogether while others are revised to fit changing circumstances [2]. Every year, you make New Year's resolutions to improve your life in some way. However, most of those intentions (goals), due to inaction, remain as just intentions and are never manifested or achieved. They just get carried over to next year's list of New Year's resolutions.

How does one control which of their intentions are manifested and which goals get left to the wind? According to Azjen and Fishbein's theory of reasoned action, human beings usually act sensibly. They take into account their circumstances, the available information, and the implications of their actions. [3]People act according to their intentions, so if we can identify the determinants of intention, then we can better predict the likeliness of an action/behavior.

The theory of reasoned action suggests two determinants of intention: (1) the attitude toward the behavior and (2) the subjective norm. The attitude toward a behavior is based on the individual's assessment (positive or negative) of performing the behavior. At the same time, the subjective norm includes all the social pressures placed on an individual to perform or not perform a behavior.

Although both determinants play roles in the probability of a particular action, the weight that each holds will depend on the individual and the intention under investigation. Regarding intention, an individual may place greater importance on their attitude toward the act rather than their perceived social obligation. However, a different individual may place greater importance on the latter instead.

Jessie, a young man of 18, has the opportunity to join the military. His father and grandfather both serve in the military and their service has always been a source of great pride for his family. Like every scenario, some pros and cons need to be considered before any action is taken. The intention under investigation here would be figuring out if joining the military is something he truly wants (desired outcome).

Based on the theory of reasoned action, Jessie possesses an attitude toward joining the military; it is either positive (likes), negative (doesn't like), or neutral (indifferent). If he has a positive attitude, he may believe, for example, that joining the military would be beneficial to his career and personal development.

If he has a negative attitude, then he probably believes the military to be too restrictive or dangerous. A neutral attitude could signify a more balanced view of the pros vs. cons or the individual's indifference toward the situation.

Understandably, someone with a positive attitude believes the outcome to be favorable and is thus more likely to engage in the associated behavior. A negative (unfavorable) attitude signifies the individual's belief in negative outcomes resulting from the associated behavior and consequently reduces the probability of engaging in the behavior.

Social pressures represent the other half of the theory of reasoned action. It considers the individual's belief that certain people/groups think they should/should not perform the behavior. Persons are more likely to engage in a behavior when social pressure supports it and less likely when social pressures oppose it.

Returning to our scenario with Jessie, his actions could either lead him to join the army or not. If he places more emphasis on his attitude, then he would likely join the army. Given his background and familial experiences, a positive attitude would have been expectedly formed. Not to say that Jessy couldn't possess a negative attitude towards joining the army, but rather less probable. Nonetheless, his negative attitude would lessen his probability of going to the army.

If he places greater importance on social pressures, he would likely join the army. Coming from a military background, he may feel great pressure to continue his family legacy and live up to the family name. On the other hand, if he believes that his family wishes him to discontinue the legacy and pursue his dreams, then that is what would be expected to occur.

In general, people are likely to perform a behavior when it is socially accepted and when they can benefit from it somehow [4]. Although both determinants contribute to the likeliness of a behavior, intentions are firmly based on the information the individual possesses.

Unveiling Intentions

An individual's action/behavior is a manifestation of their intention, while the intention is a manifestation of their beliefs and current knowledge. The theory of reasoned action follows the causal link from beliefs, through attitudes and intentions, to actual behavior. Therefore, it can be deduced that the true nature of intention lies in the information possessed (accurate or inaccurate).

Our beliefs are formed from the knowledge and experience we gain throughout our lives. Beliefs can be shared as a group or differ drastically between individuals. The quality and accuracy of the information that the individual has about the world will (indirectly) impact their behavior.

Have you ever intended to take a family vacation but couldn't afford it? The rejuvenating effects of a vacation, or rest in general, are well known. Therefore, most people would expectedly have a favorable attitude toward vacationing. What would you do if you found out that there was a 50% discount on flights to Europe this summer?

Many a vacation have hinged on information regarding discounted prices from airlines and vacation packages from hotels etc. Finding out the right information could determine whether or not your family goes to France for vacation this summer or not. The belief that vacationing was unaffordable is changed since the discounted prices make the vacation more possible

As a result of this change in beliefs due to the acquisition of new knowledge, the actions/behavior associated with the belief will certainly change as well. The idea of vacationing went from a plan to a real and now attainable goal. The resulting behavior will reflect that change from inaction due to unattainability to doing whatever is necessary for its accomplishment.

Lack of critical information during the thought process may be expressed as regret and disappointment and can be summed up with the phrase, "If I only KNEW...../ If I had known..." The more information you have on a subject, the more informed your belief and its resulting action.

The Cascading Effect

Our intentions change with time. Time awards the opportunity to develop various aspects of ourselves and to acquire new information. Some argue that the latter–the acquisition of new information–is the main catalyst for change in intention, whether it be in the form of experiential knowledge or a more conceptual or theoretical basis.

From childhood, David had always dreamed of becoming a doctor one day. He likes the idea of helping people and making a difference. However, as he gets older, with new experiences and knowledge, he decides that he no longer wants to become a doctor, and that working as a counselor would be the best way to achieve his dream (goal).

David may have realized that he becomes squeamish around blood. As a doctor, dealing with blood is a common occurrence and doctors need to develop a tolerance when dealing with it. Just as well, David finds out that it takes a much longer period of intense study to become a doctor versus other professions.

In both instances, key pieces of information, one being of a more experiential nature (squeamish) and the other based on research. Of course, experiential knowledge would take a longer time to obtain in comparison to that which can be researched in books or online. Nevertheless, in both instances, the emergence of this new information contributed greatly to David making the corresponding change.

The likelihood of new information affecting the intention-behavior relationship also depends on the confidence or strength of the intention under observation. If a person has great confidence in their intention, then the new information will rarely be sufficient to alter the planned action. Contrariwise, weakly formed intentions are easily abandoned under the scrutiny of new and/or opposing information.

It is important to note that David's goal of giving back in the previous anecdote did not change even when his intention for achieving it did. David initially believed that becoming a doctor (intention) was the best way to give back (goal/desired outcome). Due to young age, lack of experience, and knowledge, this intention would be weakly formed and more susceptible to change.

Acquiring new information caused him to reassess, and ultimately adjust his attitude and beliefs to include other occupations (i.e., counseling) as means of giving back. As a result of a weakly formed intention coupled with the acquisition of new pertinent knowledge, his intention was changed in support of this newly formed and better-formed intention.

If we revert to the theory of reasoned action, we are reminded that a change in belief would correspond with a change in attitude and, ultimately, in revised intention. There may be more than one way to achieve a goal. Doing your due diligence in information research and acquisition opens up more avenues for achieving your goals. You could say that information is the map that guides action.

Action Steps

Controlled action is not as simple as knowing what you are doing. There are many considerations surrounding action or lack thereof, so as usual, one must start with understanding the concept before being able to truly apply it.

All actions are controlled, or more correctly, should be controlled. The concept of control doesn't only include the conscious management of our mental, physical or emotional faculties but the nonconscious management as well.

Nonconscious management involves cognitive processes that get repetitively managed to the extent that they no longer need to be consciously managed. They signify an almost ever-present intent to attain the desired results.

For instance, you decide to wake up at 5:00 a.m., an hour earlier, every day to exercise and hopefully improve your health. At first, you may find it difficult to wake up even with the alarm blaring in your ear, but with time and consistent effort, it becomes easier for your body to wake up (adaptation). Eventually, your body will wake at 5 whether you want it to or not (nonconscious management).

Without the adequate motivation and effort, waking up remains a difficult task requiring more conscious management. Prolonged difficulty with waking up will eventually lead to giving up on the intention altogether (abandonment).

The nonconscious nature of our mental process does not signify a lack of control but the very opposite, mastery.

Control comes from the awareness of the conscious and nonconscious cognitive processes and their effective management, whether in the form of adaptation/abandonment.

1. Clearly define intentions: Actions are derived from intention. Specific intention cultivates specific action. In basketball, for example, the difference between a good shooter and a great one could be the lack of a clearly defined intent.

When training to be a shooter, a good shooter takes 100 shots at the rim and scores maybe 50. He intends to score as many as possible (vague intention). Some shots hit the rim, some hit the backboard, and some don't hit either.

A great shooter takes 100 shots at a specific spot on the rim, not just in that general direction, and scores 80. He intended to score 90 baskets (specific intention). Knowing that there is little room for error, the shooter knows every shot counts and takes full advantage of every shot, exerting full effort and focus with every shot.

Clearly defining the corresponding shot will also be more defined and specific, increasing your chances of success.

The same principle can be applied to any intention, whether weight loss, learning, or business decisions. Are you intent on losing some weight? How much? Do you want to be more educated? In what field? Do you want a raise at work? How much of a raise?

You arrive at your destination faster when you know where you are going.

2. Understanding short and long-term goals: Some intentions are more feasible than others at a given time; therefore, some goals are better suited for the long term rather than the short. For example, weight loss would be considered a long-term goal, whereas drinking eight glasses of water daily would be more of a short-term nature.

Understanding that long-term goals comprise multiple short-term goals, we can begin to manage them better. Furthermore, it discourages us from trying to attain a long-term goal too quickly.

Undoubtedly, feelings of anxiety, frustration, and even health problems would arise if sudden weight loss occurred for whatever reason (physical, mental or social). If the focus is shifted from the long-term goal to achieving its more attainable short-term counterparts, then feelings of accomplishment will motivate continued progress and achievement of the long-term goal.

You feel good when you realize you drank 10 glasses today when your goal was eight or if you exercised for an hour like you had planned. These small wins (accomplishments) encourage the individual toward their long-term goal of weight loss. Focusing solely on the long-term goal of weight loss may not be beneficial, especially since you haven't lost any weight from the last time you weighed yourself this morning.

Short-term goals are more readily obtainable than long-term goals. Keep your long-term goals in mind, and even though you may not be able to obtain them due to lack of information or opportunity, etc., focus on the more achievable short-term objectives.

As the quote attributed to Hoda Kotb goes: "Life is a series of baby steps."

<u>Key Reader Takeaways</u>

- Specificity of knowledge and intent leads to better productivity.
- The mind controls and the body follows. Take control of your thought and better manage their processes when the opportunity is presented.

3

THE PSYCHOLOGY OF PERFORMANCE
IMPROVEMENT

The Right Time

Whenever time is a factor (which is always) for determining performance, time management naturally becomes a vital skill for achieving your goal. In one way or another, we have all been exposed to some type of time management system and thus, to some extent, are aware of the benefits of managing your time well. The limited nature of time alone is enough to warrant further investigation into managing it more effectively.

The education system, for example, uses various time management systems to ensure that students learn as much as possible in the limited time they are at school. Time is managed on a macro and micro level–from how many days of school are assigned for classes to how many periods and classes can be taught in one day. By establishing time parameters for achieving the goal of student education, guidelines can be created that ensure that only the most suitable/effective strategies are implemented.

Consider the thought process of a teacher for example. A teacher knows that classes are usually about an hour long. Since one hour is not enough to effectively teach a particular subject, the lesson is broken down into segments that will be taught over the next classes. In knowing how much time was needed to teach the topic comprehensively and how much time was available for teaching, the teacher could implement strategies to overcome both these time restrictions and ultimately attain the goal of topic edification.

As the famous saying attributed to Napoleon Hill so succinctly puts it, "A goal is a dream with a deadline." Cognizance of time as a restriction (e.g., deadlines, time durations, etc.) can guide the amount of effort, frequency, and even the motivation for achieving your goal. Mentioning time as a factor in achievement may seem redundant, but it is in its awareness and consideration that one can truly begin to reap the benefits of its application.

Have you ever set goals for yourself yet never achieved them? Weight loss, for instance, is a common goal that many people set for themselves. The focus is on the weight loss itself: How much weight should I lose? From which part of my body? Am I overweight, or is it my body type? Some even go as far as targeting a particular outfit to be worn after the weight loss.

We often overemphasize the GOAL that we set and not HOW to go about achieving that goal. Consequently, we struggle greatly because not enough time and thought are given to planning and strategizing. Although it is beneficial to know what one is working towards, it's reassuring and more valuable to know that you have a full-proof plan for achieving said goal.

Strategizing is only half the battle. Another important aspect of time management is procrastination. For some individuals, failure to achieve their goal is not due to the spontaneous or reactive use of their time but to failure to implement their strategy on time.

Improved time management skills are a proven way to increase your productivity. There is considerable research on time management skills and practices, but there is another way entirely to approach goal achievement and improved performance.

Similar to how a doctor would approach healing the body, so too should one address the issues of a psychological nature. Instead of treating the symptoms of procrastination, which will most likely reoccur later in life, one should treat the cause.

Behind The Scenes

Procrastination refers to the delaying or putting off something. For many, this phenomenon is not novel. However, more consideration needs to be placed on the cause(s) for procrastination.

As the time afforded for completing a task diminishes, the pressures increase. Procrastination is a burdensome process that can be traced back to both internal (individual) and external (societal) causes. It involves systematically adding more pressure on the individual to achieve their goal, either self-inflicted or environmentally imposed.

Several studies have shown that anxiety [1], depression [2], and worry [3] are associated with procrastinatory behavior [4]. These negative feelings are components of the metacognitive experiences associated with the topic or behavior. The resulting attempts at self-regulation, therefore, will be greatly influenced by these feelings.

If you analyze self-regulated learning–for instance, when a student feels difficulty or detects an error–a negative affect is also experienced. However, it is often the case that the student cannot readily identify the source of this feeling [5]. Understanding the source of this feeling provides valuable information as to how and if it can be addressed or rectified.

An error in processing can be traced back to various sources, including: (1) task demands: what needs to be done (2) declarative and procedural knowledge: knowledge and experience on the topic (3) ability: physical and mental limitations, and (4) conflict: discrepancies between previous and current knowledge, to name a few. Depending on which category the error occurred, the best suitable action, if any, would undoubtedly differ.

For example, John decides to build a webpage to advertise his profile and experience. He has a vision for the site and believes that he is the best person to bring his idea to reality. However, he experiences negative feelings concerning him being the one to undertake this endeavor. One possible source for the negative affect could be that John doesn't know anything about website design so he wouldn't know where to begin. Another source could be that John doesn't currently own his own computer, although he has taken numerous website development courses.

The way that John would attempt to handle each situation would understandably differ. In the first scenario, John could sign-up for some web development classes or, reluctantly enough, work closely with an already skilled web designer. In the latter scenario, John could purchase/rent a device with which he could do all his designing.

In the previous scenarios, we can appreciate the value of the metacognitive processes in identifying the source of negative affect and suitable strategies for alleviating them. Subsequently, goals become more attainable in reality and, more importantly, in the mind of the individual.

In the spirit of appreciation, it would be remiss not to discuss the driving force or reason behind undertaking any endeavor. After all, we are goal driven species in that our actions usually have a preferred outcome. This form of achievement goal orientation also has a notable part to play in improving performance.

Gas or Diesel: What Drives You?

The concept of orientation is centered on the basic attitude and beliefs a person possesses toward a topic. With achievement goal orientation, an individual focuses on the pursued result of the learning process [6]. For instance, you are reading this book in hopes that on its completion, you will have improved and expanded thinking ability or, at the very least, the means for obtaining it [7].

Ultimately, the focus is on the final goal trying to be achieved and reaping the associated rewards. Depending on the achievement goal, the type of thinking and methodology employed for attaining said results would naturally differ[8]. Researchers have proposed two contrasting achievement goals: mastery goals [9] and performance goals [10].

People with mastery goals believe that performance is directly correlated with the effort put into it. Their focus is on laying a solid foundation of knowledge and understanding on the topic and increasing competence. This type of person likes a challenge. They seek out challenges as they are seen as opportune for challenging or solidifying their savvy and know-how on the topic.

On the other hand, people with performance goals strive to demonstrate their competence and avoid negative judgments of their competence [11]. What concerns these people is how their skill and competence are perceived by others, especially when viewed in a negative light. As a result, they avoid non-essential challenges for fear of exposing any inefficiencies or escaping negative judgments.

When faced with failure, people with mastery goals maintain a positive affect and become even more solution-oriented. In contrast, people with performance goals will withdraw, experience negative affect, and lose interest, perhaps due to the increased chance of failure associated with difficulty.

For example, John has always wanted to be a famous guitarist and tour the world. He started guitar lessons at 12 and so commenced his journey to rock and roll stardom. John is not as skilled as other popular guitarists, so he doesn't get many gigs.

At that point, John has a decision to make based on the information that he currently has about himself and the situation. If John possesses mastery goals, then he doesn't get discouraged and instead increases his effort (becomes motivated) and bolsters his understanding and skills to a more comparable level and beyond. On the contrary, if John possesses only performance goals, he will experience negative affect and could give up on the guitar, learn another instrument, or give up on his dream entirely.

Achievement goal orientation, mastery, and performance can be further divided by two distinct factors: approach and avoidance. The mastery-approach involves working to attain positive results, whereas mastery-avoidance shuns negative outcomes [12].Furthermore, the performance-approach aim to demonstrate competence while performance-avoidance focuses on avoiding demonstrations of incompetence [13].

The positive relationship between mastery goals and metacognition has been thoroughly researched [14151617]. Students with mastery goals prioritize monitoring their learning, are more open to feedback, and aren't easily overcome by negative circumstances [18]. Conversely, research on the relationship between the performance approach and metacognition is ambiguous. Research shows that performance-avoidance goals are negatively related to metacognition [19].

Achievement goal orientation reveals the underlying motivators and influencers for pursuing or abandoning a project. A cognizant approach to your thinking consistently produces positive results. Reevaluating your orientation could be the X factor to get you back on track and more motivated.

The Mental Stylist

People have preferences in music, food, movies, and pretty much any other category where options exist. For various reasons, people are almost instinctively drawn to things that complement their way of thinking, that are relatable or produce in themselves an overall positive affect.

For example, people with similar preferences, thinking, or behavior will be drawn together and are more likely to get along. In school, there would be the cool kids, the jocks, the nerds, etc.

One perspective, based on parallel reasoning, focuses on the effect of the style that learners adopt on performance improvement. Research has identified three distinct styles: (1) deep processing, (2) surface processing, and (3) disorganization.

As the name suggests, deep processing is the most elaborative approach to the learning process. It involves the constant verification of new information with a particular focus on subject comprehension. People using deep processing become familiar with a topic and better adapt and apply knowledge. Deep processing is the most successful approach to learning and can also be called critical thinking [20].

Surface processing results in difficulty and, oftentimes, failure to fully grasp the nature of the information. This unfavorable outcome is not only due to a lack of comprehension of the information but also because the learning process is based on the ability to recall the information rather than understanding its nature.

In preparing for an examination with limited time, cramming is a popular strategy for encoding information. Someone using this strategy may successfully recall the information but cannot apply that information to a particular situation for the desired result.

The least effective learning style is disorganization, an almost freestyle-ish approach to learning. With no apparent organization or structure of information, there is minimal chance of beneficial information processing and understanding its value.

A significant amount of research supports claims that mastery goals are positive predictors of deep processing and performance goals of surface processing [21,22,23,24,25]. Furthermore, researchers have shown a positive correlation (as one increases the other increases) between deep processing and performance results and a negative correlation (as one increases the other decreases), or none at all, between surface processing and performance results [26,27].

The style of learning used is highly dependent on the metacognitive skills possessed and employed[28]. For example, Schoenfeld explained that novice learners don't give much consideration to strategy selection and employ the seemingly first appropriate strategy that comes to mind[29]. On the other hand, individuals employing metacognitive skills will determine the best suitable approach before beginning and are even able to abandon or adapt their strategy if required [30].

Fashion combines the best parts of different styles to create a new and original product. Thinking is no different. Combine different elements of different styles and create your unique style for doing things.

Action Steps

Similar to the conscious and deliberate way we manage our finite resources like oil, so too should we approach the use of our faculties, time, and effort. Individuals must assume the role of a manager and use available resources to maximize output and reap the associated rewards (performance improvement).

Business magnate Frederick W. Smith reputedly said, "A manager is not a person who can do the work better than his men; he is a person who can get his men to do the work better than he can."

Not everyone is cut out or even wants to possess a managerial position. Management usually involves increased responsibility and a wider purview. At the same time, management has the ability and means to affect serious change and acquire more substantial rewards. A manager (you/your mind) uses those in their employ (metacognitive skills) to accomplish a goal.

For improved performance, one must become an effective manager of time, effort, and focus. These concepts are interrelated and interdependent; therefore, poor management in one area will affect other areas as well. For instance, your lack of time to prepare for a test causes you to focus on only the important topics or those believed to appear on the test. Less time also means increased effort to achieve a goal.

1. Manage your time: As Steven R. Covey so correctly said, "The key is in not spending time, but in investing it." When you view the use of your time as an investment, then you automatically expect a reward or return. You invest depending on the possibility for and magnitude of the associated reward.

If you are going to bet on a team, it's safe to say you would select based on which team had the best chance of winning and not on the fact that their team's Jersey is blue, which is your favorite color. Take the time to set goals and deadlines, take the time to choose and employ the best strategies, and take the time to reflect and reevaluate when necessary. Although it may seem counterintuitive, taking the time to do these things will save you time in the long run.

2. Manage your effort and focus: Understanding what drives your effort and awareness of the expected outcome can greatly assist in managing your effort, its frequency, and magnitude. Even the methodology employed can depend on how much effort the individual has available or devoted to attaining a goal. Effort squandered, on the other hand, leads to feelings of frustration and exhaustion.

If you have always wanted to be a veterinarian, then there is no effort too great in making your dream a reality. You would move to a new place, study for most of your days and not have much of a social life if that was what it took to accomplish your goal.

On the other hand, if your parents always wanted you to be a veterinarian and you reluctantly decide to follow that path, then the effort you put in will be significantly reduced. Consequently producing poor results and increased difficulty in attaining the goal.

You expend effort based on what you are focused on. Spend more time focusing on HOW to attain your goal rather than WHAT the intended goal/outcome should be.

3. Understand your mental tendencies: When you begin to understand your thinking better, you will start to notice trends or patterns. Circumstances that may work to your benefit and those that are counterproductive. For example, your mind may be clearer and more focused in the morning. As a result, you get the most work done during that morning period.

Conversely, you feel tired and your mind gets foggy in the afternoon. You struggle to complete an assignment. Being aware of this mental tendency will allow an individual to organize the bulk of his work to be done in the morning and the less prioritized work in the afternoon. Undoubtedly, more would be accomplished.

4. Define your orientation: Do you work for a deeper understanding and competence on the subject matter or are you more concerned with the way others perceive your competence and skill? There are situations where it may be valuable to display your ability to others, like evaluations, interviews, and many other competitive

arenas. However, performance-driven learning is surface deep and usually includes minimal knowledge or skill since it's based on perception. Mastery goals, on the other hand, are based on understanding and foster deep understanding and thus better use.

5. Embrace different styles: Our style defines us. The way we move, speak, and even think. Our style is the culmination of bits and pieces of different styles constructed in a particular way. That's why everyone's style is unique. That being said, even though the final products are unique and special, the individual components have a similar makeup, but are organized and applied differently.

Although you embrace your style and identify with it, your usual style in clothes, for example, may not be appropriate for attending a formal dining event where you might be looking for investors. Yes, you could still attend the event but issues will undoubtedly arise in people's minds and even in your own. Not to say that your style wouldn't be appreciated, but without speaking to you, people may begin to form impressions and make assumptions that may interfere with your chances of landing investors. Flexibility is important.

Not every concept needs to be deeply processed. Some situations call for a more disorganized approach, or more correctly, less processed, and more felt or experienced. People don't usually have a systematic approach to art or having fun, but that's where the beauty lies.

We get bits and pieces of information from our experience, from research, and even our genetics that help form our learning styles. Do not be limited by one style through its particular allure. Deep processing yields the greatest results but requires the most effort. Disorganization produces the least results but requires minimal effort. The choice is yours.

Key Reader Takeaways

- Time, effort, and focus can be great indicators of performance.
- Be your manager: Manage your time, effort, and focus.
- Find out what drives you: Mastery or Performance.
- Adapt or fail: Adaptation is a central concept for the survival of any species. As humans with cognitive abilities, we should also be able to adapt our minds to suit the situation and surrounding circumstances. Bruce Lee once said, "Be water, my friend."

4

SELF-EFFICACY: REALITY VS. PERCEPTION

Amidst times of thought and decision, it is not uncommon to have an inner dialogue with oneself. After all, who knows you better than yourself? You weigh options, compare pros and cons, and reason out a conclusion.

In cartoons, when a character is faced with a dilemma of an ethical nature, for example, a small angel and a small devil appear on their opposite shoulders. As the character debates a course of action, their new advisors make opposing proposals.

Both proposals are based on information that the character possesses and not on any unique or crucial information either entity possesses. The character's action/choice depends on which entity makes the more persuasive argument.

This well-known setup is representative of the mind as it weighs factors like desire, ability, and results during the decision-making process. The mind can be very persuasive and the subsequent action(s) taken may differ drastically from person to person, even when faced with the same or similar circumstances. Studies suggest that the decision-making process is not merely an expression of knowledge or skill [1], but rather an individually unique method of processing information from the context of experience [2].

Certain contributors play a more significant role in the decision-making process including metacognitive skills, priorities, and self-efficacy (perceived ability). The importance of metacognition has already been established. Moreover, prioritization is mostly a subjective process, and consequently, priorities will vary from person to person for different reasons.

Self-efficacy refers to a person's perceived ability to gain the desired outcome by taking necessary steps [3]. Like metacognition, self-efficacy can be improved, and thus it is within this variable that another chance for personal development emerges.

Returning to the initial angel versus devil analogy, suppose that our character's name is Amanda and her metacognitive skills are limited. One can imagine the argument between her newly acquired advisors being a pretty short one.

As Amanda decides on whether or not to attend a late-night concert with her friends, her adversarial shoulder counsels begin to dispute and persuade based on the information that she possesses.

They mostly debate the time and location of the concert since that's all Amanda bothered to ask about: her priorities. "Don't go it's too far/late," says one advisor, "Go, it's not too far/late," says the other, and that would be the end of it.

Now, what Amanda isn't aware of is that her favorite band of all time will be performing there as well. If Amanda had possessed this key bit of information from the start, then it would have been a different kind of debate.

With a limited ability to process the information effectively, her decision-making would naturally rely on other factors like her priorities and ability to follow through with her decision (self-efficacy). Her lack of metacognitive skills prevents her from seeing the situation from different perspectives and hence, limits her chances for success. Furthermore, via metacognitive experience, negative feelings could arise associated with difficulty in trying to deal with the situation and further hinder the thought process.

Studies have shown that the relationship between self-efficacy and performance is partially mediated by metacognition [4]. The perceived difficulty in dealing with the situation practically forces her to settle for the less prioritized/optimal outcome. In a contradictory fashion, the perceived ability to achieve the sub-optimal outcome (optimal in her mind, however, due to the absence or improper use of metacognition) will increase her chances of success.

Self-Efficacy

Understanding the role of negative affect on hindering thinking is only half the conversation. We should also consider the role of a positive affect and belief in the way we think.

Winnie, on the other hand, possesses adequate metacognitive skills and therefore has a more wholesome understanding of her situation and the relevant contributing factors. She takes advantage of these skills by prioritizing well for the best outcome. Although she may be aware of all the steps needed to move forward, her actions are still heavily determined by her perceived ability to attain it (self-efficacy).

For example, Winnie goes to do some grocery shopping. She is deciding on what kind of laundry detergent to buy. One brand is cheaper but less effective. The other is more expensive but does a better overall job. Winnie prioritizes the efficiency of the detergent over the cost, so she wants to buy the more expensive one. However, Winnie has a budget for groceries, and buying the more expensive option could put her over it.

If Winnie has strong beliefs that she could find a way to fit the detergent she wants into the budget, then her metacognitive skills will greatly assist her in finding a way to adjust the budget or its components to accommodate the change. On the other hand, if Winnie's belief in her ability to adjust the budget adequately is weak, she would more likely decide to buy the cheaper detergent instead.

Bandura and Wood reveal that investigation and problem resolution are the main focuses for people who possess a strong sense of self-efficacy, while those with a weak sense concern themselves more with performance evaluation. Success depends on optimistic self-efficacy beliefs in one's abilities to achieve desired outcomes [5].

Winnie's focus is on finding a way to get the detergent she wants (resolution) and not on her ability to manipulate the budget (evaluation). In her mind, the dilemma is more concerned with HOW to go about including the detergent rather than IF the detergent could be purchased with the available budget.

The absence of a structured thinking approach, through the effective use of metacognitive skills, allows the mind to be swayed to less optimal outcomes. You cannot use what you do not possess, and you cannot improve on what has not been done. Moreover, the perceived ability of an individual to achieve a goal can serve as a strong motivator for doing or not going something.

Rome Wasn't Built In A Day

Imagine your mind to be a beautiful and vast library, a collection of understandings, knowledge of beliefs, experiential data, etc. You are the chief librarian and therefore responsible for locating requested books (information) if any.

There should be an organized system in the way that these books are stored and retrieved (encoded). As one grows their library collections, so too must one improve the system for storage and retrieval. A library containing 50 books will be much easier to manage than one comprised of 500, therefore the current system in place, if any, would need to be improved.

Every thought or situation, is like a visitor to your library, attempting to find valuable insight into their particular circumstances. As the chief librarian, you should guide the visitor to exactly where they need to go. Instead of guesswork or relying on memory, you employ the system and locate the relevant information.

Familiarity with the library system also plays a role in the ability to find and subsequently use a book. Every librarian needs to be trained and familiarized with the particular system being used in their library. If not, then feelings of frustration and anxiety are likely to surface.

Organized thought is one of the best strategies for solving a problem or dealing with a situation. Schemas are the building blocks of our thinking, understanding, and recollection. They form the skeletal or basic structure of our mind and therefore shapes our thought.

These representative models and theories (schema) guide our thinking. The stronger the schema, the more likely it will hold up under the scrutiny of varied circumstances.

For example, it would be contradictory to see an atheist in church worshipping God. In the same way, the extent of your faith will also affect the corresponding actions, like whether you go to church every Sunday or once in a while.

Schemata are formed over time and can be revised with additional knowledge and experience. Similarly, metacognition improves with age, with children and adolescents having poor metacognition relative to adults [6]. Schemata are used to make informed metacognitive assessments and are thus important in both the learning and self-regulatory processes.

Similar to how running, an act that most can do, can be improved with training, so too can we improve the quality of our schemata through training. Investigators have shown that both children and adults can be readily trained to use representations, strategies, and knowledge [7] to comprehend information, solve problems and regulate their cognitive processes [8].

Schema training involves developing cognitive structures that assist in information processing comprehension. Brown, Campione, and Day identified three types of training that could aid in the advancement of metacognitive knowledge and schema training: Blind, Informed, and Self-control [9].

Blind training involves instigating the use of a strategy without a proper explanation of its use. This kind of training is commonly used by children and young learners as their knowledge and skills are limited. A trial-and-error approach for obtaining new skills, blind training may succeed in acquiring a new skill but fails in providing the supporting context on its application.

Informed training, on the other hand, encourages the use of strategy with an understanding of its significance. Learners who employ self-control training are aware of and monitor their mental processes and skills. They know when, why, and how to use strategies effectively.

Self-control training has proved effective in promoting self-sufficiency while improving the learner's performance. As a result, they rely less on external cues embedded in instruction and more on their awareness when implementing strategies [10].

For example, when learning the sequence of the colors of the rainbow, learners are often taught the acronym ROYGBIV representing red, orange, yellow, green, blue, indigo and violet respectively. By remembering this much easier-to-recall acronym, students can now correctly recollect the sequence of colors thus achieving the target goal. Recollection is the extent of their mastery and is a good example of blind training.

Instead of learning a particular acronym in the hopes of proper recall, students should acquire knowledge of the acronym system and its application. If learners are introduced to the concept of acronyms as a means of compacting information in word form rather than as a means of remembering one particular acronym, then learners are more likely to maintain and reuse that strategy.

In doing so, individuals are more likely to retain and maintain the use of said strategy in varied circumstances. Learners will likely apply the learned strategy to similar situations where sequence recollection is a factor.

Learners applying the acronym method to situations outside of sequence recollection is one way to demonstrate self-control training. Another display of self-control training would be learners realizing that the acronym method is best used with shorter or small bits of information. The longer the acronym, the harder it is to remember.

Schemata are used as tools for learning. Quality tools produce superior results. One of the main goals of learning is transfer. Transfer refers to the application of a trained strategy to dissimilar learning tasks, problems, or circumstances. Transfer is an essential concept if learners are to acquire independence and self-sufficiency.

Generally, detached strategies provide the best likelihood of training transfer in that they are neither content-specific nor likely to be associated only with particular lesson content [11]. Instead of strictly focusing on the problem at hand, focus on selecting and applying the best strategies.

Training your mind to create and apply quality schemata takes time but the results will be unquestionable. Students who develop metacognitive skills are far more likely to be able to make the changes needed in their study habits and learning strategies when faced with unfamiliar tasks or challenges than students who do not [12].

Like pyramids and castles of ancient architecture, quality schemata might take a long time to be built, but they stand the test of time with flying colors.

Turning On The Cruise Control

One of the fondest memories many people have is of learning how to ride a bicycle. From crash landing every two feet to riding without hands, the process of learning to ride a bike is a good illustration of the conscious and nonconscious processes occurring in the mind.

At first, riding a bike seems like a complicated procedure that requires great skills and aptitude. This may be intimidating for many and, understandably, self-doubt may arise. Your processing of information is very much on a conscious level, fully utilizing your working memory. Your working memory is comparable to the RAM system in computers. The more RAM, the more processing power.

Every movement is critically monitored and analyzed as one tries to manage various stimuli in real-time and implement the corresponding reaction. The focus is totally on the moment as a lot of processing power is required to coordinate an appropriate response.

You are barely able to process your name being called out as you indiscriminately head toward the garbage cans.

Practice and experience play crucial factors in learning and acquiring new skills, but the conscious management of these mental processes is key. As improvements occur, the management of each of these processes becomes more automated, allowing more processing power to be attributed where necessary. These now automated (fully/semi) processes are still being processed but now on a nonconscious level.

Soon, practically all of these processes will become automated and individuals can even handle additional tasks with the now freed-up working memory of the conscious mind. Learning to drive follows a similar process, as eventually drivers no longer "think" about driving and just drive. At the same time, they can have conversations, listen to the radio, and even enjoy the scenery.

There is no doubt a conscious and nonconscious aspect to the mind. Similar to how one manages physical stimuli and feedback from oneself and the environment, so too does one manage the cognitive processes governing the mind. We can therefore argue that this management system also possesses conscious and nonconscious elements.

Research shows that people monitor and regulate their cognition without being consciously aware of it [13]. Additional research suggests that metacognition is instrumental in the regulation of attention and effort [14]. Irrespective of the greater contributor, the focus lies on the relationship between them.

There is a connection between the conscious and nonconscious nature (and management) of cognitive processes. Nonconscious processes have their roots in conscious processes. Similarly, the management of these processes, initially conscious, becomes automated with time and experience (nonconscious).

This process of automation is usually one-sided in that it should be succeeded by some form of mastery. However, there are instances where nonconscious (automated) processes can return to being consciously processed once more. When a situation cannot be resolved by the automated management system, then the nature of the management becomes a conscious one. This is a pivotal moment for either solidifying your belief in your management system or improving it.

Conscious And Nonconscious Fluidity

While driving your car every day, you are faced with a plethora of stimuli and information that is monitored and processed by your nonconscious management system in real-time. You see a speed bump ahead, you begin to slow down yet continue to converse with your passenger. The light turns green on the traffic light and you accelerate while listening to the GPS directions. Even with varied stimuli, the nonconscious management system can easily deal with the respective situation.

On the other hand, while driving on a snowy day, you approach a speed bump and attempt to slow down but don't. At that point, the nature of your now nonconscious management system begins to become a conscious one. You may even pump the breaks again to verify the discrepancy in the outcome.

If that doesn't work, then doubt arises in the validity and effectiveness of the management system (metacognitive feeling) and you begin to consciously think about the driving process. You test the steering, check for power and consider all elements that could be affecting the expected outcome of the driving processes. The driver is super alert and likely in an almost panicked state.

As soon as you determine the slippery road to be the source of the discrepancy, then you adjust your driving accordingly and immediately begin to feel a sense of relief (metacognitive experience). Moreover, an experienced driver would not assume the discrepancy to originate from an error in the conscious or unconscious monitoring systems but rather from external factors like the vehicle and weather, allowing it to be located and dealt with more efficiently.

The aforementioned scenario reinforced the driver's belief in his cognitive processing and its subsequent monitoring whether conscious or nonconscious by nature. Nevertheless, overemphasis on the validity of strategies and systems of thought can lead to maladaptive tendencies, oversight, and increased complication.

An overconfident driver would continue to drive in his usual way at his usual speed knowing that if he encounters any issues due to the inclement road conditions, then he could handle it. Moreover, if the driver had already dealt with similar situations in the past, then he could have a false sense of safety.

Not to say that the driver would not be skilled enough to handle whatever mother nature would throw at him, but wouldn't it be a better decision to err on the side of caution even with a supreme belief in your driving skills?

We are faced with many situations that test our thought. We receive new information and gather new experiences that create and test our schema. Conscious cognitive processing could signify the lack of mastery, lack of knowledge, or an error in processing especially if it had been previously governed by a nonconscious management system.

If we allow our beliefs, no matter how sound the foundation, to be open to change, then a corresponding change will also take place in the way that we think, perceive and act.

Action Steps

Take control of your thinking by understanding its framework and what affects it.

<u>1. Perception is ONE key</u>: Self-efficacy is based on the perception of one's abilities and not on the actuality or effectiveness of their use. Just because you believe you can do something, doesn't mean that you can achieve something that you never thought possible.

A person's self-efficacy should be based on their experience and capabilities. However, not everyone perceives success in the same way. We gain experience at different speeds and for different reasons.

Although our self-efficacy provides valuable feedback as to the likelihood of success, remember that it is not the only factor to consider when making decisions. The only way to truly know is to do it. Even with failure, valuable knowledge is gained. It's not that you can't do it, it's that you can't do it YET.

<u>2. Become a defense attorney</u>: It's not uncommon for a person to have an opinion about something or make allegations, but when you do, there needs to be evidence to support it. In the same way, people also need to be able to defend their beliefs when necessary.

Like a lawyer, it takes time to build a case, gather proof, interview witnesses, etc.

Don't base your belief on assumptions, hearsay, and propaganda. Base schemata on factual and verifiable information when possible so that when your mind is presented with any questionable cases, your beliefs can be properly defended.

3. Test your schemata: Unfortunately, it takes a precarious predicament for people to occur before people assess their beliefs. We all have belief in some form or another, but sometimes, that belief is not necessarily warranted.

The most effective way to find out is to test your beliefs yourself. Put yourself in situations that test the validity of your schemata. By doing this from time to time, you allow yourself to strengthen, update, or adapt schemata.

4. Recognize growth opportunities: Many opportunities are not capitalized upon due to a lack of recognition or presence of mind. We often recognize an opportunity after the fact. Become more present in the decision-making process to allow yourself the chance for personal growth. As hockey hall of famer Wayne Gretzky stated, "You miss 100% of the shots you don't take."

Key Reader Takeaways

- Belief is an extraordinary motivator. Leverage belief to embrace failure and develop self-efficacy based on actual experience and capabilities.
- Choose quality over quantity when forming schemata.
- Thinking has a conscious and nonconscious nature that can indicate the mastery of actions or the necessity of skill improvement.
- Training and testing provide valuable feedback on improving thinking.

5

ENVIRONMENTAL CULTIVATION

On the first day of high school, Smith wakes up early and gets ready for the day. He is a straight-A student and enjoys learning new things. In class, Smith raises his hand in an attempt to respond to every question posed. Most of the time he answers correctly, thus reassuring his belief in his abilities and motivating his progress. Smith is an ideal learner since he possesses the right attitude and high confidence in his skills.

Unfortunately, Smith is not very popular in class. Some students see him as a showoff while others may dislike him because his "excellent" behavior reflects badly on them. Consequently, Smith is treated differently and becomes a social pariah. His sense of well-being is negatively affected. This disturbance may manifest as sadness, depression, loss of focus, loss of appetite, decreased performance, etc.

In an attempt to redeem his social standing, Smith no longer raises his hand to ask or answer questions and minimalizes his class participation. Gradually he is accepted back into good social graces and treated like any other member of the micro-society. His performance increases, he makes more friends, and stabilizes his moods and overall well-being.

Thought and learning do not exist in a social vacuum and, as such, are susceptible to social impacts. We have all behaved or not behaved in certain ways to appease the social norms of our circumstances. It is imperative to be aware of and understand the relationship between psychosocial needs and performance.

Needs Umbrella

Research shows the fulfillment of psychosocial needs to be essential to positive functioning [1] and well-being [2,3]. These needs can be of a social or physical nature and will affect the psychology of an individual if left unsatisfied. In particular, the need for close relationships and respect from others have the greatest impact on happiness and well-being [4].

Research surrounding social needs proposes one overall social needs umbrella that encompasses all other social variables and circumstances [5]. For example, the need for approval and the need for power could be considered derivatives of a larger need, the need to belong, and falls under its umbrella.

This mass grouping of social needs does nothing to determine which social need is associated with what kind of behavior or performance. Imagine a car being moved by ten men—two at the front, two at the back, and three on each side of the car. These men are of different strengths and at different positions, thus contributing at varying degrees.

It suffices to say, ten men aren't needed to push a car. Identifying and managing the key contributors will increase the efficiency of the entire process. By identifying the two men at the back of the car to be the greatest contributors, we understand better the consequences of their absence and at the same time understand their relationship with the other eight men in their joint venture.

The Social Production Function (SPF) Theory distinguishes three basic social needs and two basic physical needs as key factors in the psychosocial realm [6]. The basic physical needs include comfort and stimulation, while the social needs comprise affection, behavioral confirmation, and status.

Physical comfort is attained when the body is not hungry, thirsty, or in any discomfort. The individual feels relaxed and stress levels are reduced to a minimum. Stimulation, on the other hand, is quite the opposite in that excitement and arousal are the desired outcomes. Physically speaking, we interpret stimuli from the body that lets us know which one we need: comfort or stimulation.

On the other hand, one also receives stimuli from the environment and people. Status concerns your relative social standing, affection pertains to feelings of acceptance and love, and behavioral confirmation relates to the feeling of being a functional contributor, especially in the eyes of other important people.

In terms of social needs, if an individual can identify the satisfier of these social demands, then more control is obtained in the way and extent by which the environment affects them. Research has identified various social relationships and situations as satisfiers of these social needs. The key lies in the type and quality of relationships that individuals have between themselves and their social environment.

The need for affection is satisfied by relationships that foster love, empathy, and understanding expressed physically or emotionally. The need for behavioral confirmation is satisfied by relationships that appreciate the value of an individual's contribution and promote a good self-image. Lastly, the need for status is fulfilled by relationships that make individuals feel respected and accomplished.

Putting It All Together

From an evolutionary psychology school of thought, the way that these social needs and satisfiers are manifested will differ across time but serve the same function. For instance, the need for status can be traced back to the more primal pursuit of domination; packs have leaders that have proven their value to the pack and earned their respect and associated benefits.

Affection has its roots in the maternal and paternal instincts of the individual. Affection promotes bonding between parent and child and fosters trust and strengthens bonds. Strong bonds signify more of a willingness to communicate and cooperate, therefore increasing one's chances of survival.

Behavioral confirmation, in evolutionary terms, provides validation for being part of a group or pack. In a troop of monkeys and every primate group, you can find an alpha male (as well as an alpha female). The alpha male is responsible for leading and protecting the pack. If other males question the alpha's ability to carry out his responsibility, then he will be challenged and a fight for validation will occur. The actions and outcome of the fight will determine if the other monkeys continue to accept him as the alpha or instate a new one[7].

Similar analogies can be drawn with human beings within a social context. For instance, the Maasai of Kenya and Tanzania have boys go through a series of rites of passage. This ceremony or act signifies and solidifies the individual's place within the group. It is only at this time that they are accepted into the group as men and are no longer considered boys. As men now, they have different roles and responsibilities within their group or society[8].

In a more "developed" society, the way that these social needs are expressed and met will differ, but their importance to individual well-being and performance remains constant. For people to perform at their best, the fulfillment of social needs is essential [9]. Similar to Maslow's research on the hierarchy of needs, optimal performance cannot be achieved if more basic needs are not being met.

It is quite difficult to calculate the result of an equation when you are weak from hunger. It is difficult to lend a sympathetic ear when you are dealing with heartache. It's difficult to work with people who believe that you didn't earn your position but inherited it. Physical, emotional, or social imbalances can have negative effects on the individual well-being.

While preexisting conditions and predispositions may heavily determine physical and emotional imbalances, an individual's social environment is within their control, at least to some extent. Therefore it would be prudent to focus on the types and quality of the social relations that people inevitably form. Furthermore, determining whether or not your social needs are being met provides useful feedback that can be used to adjust or reinforce behaviors.

These social needs will carry different weights depending on the individual. Research based on SPF Theory shows the role of demographic variables in the social needs pursued; with gender, women focus more on fulfilling affection needs while men prioritize status needs fulfillment [10]. Consequently, the individual's sense of well-being will be affected to the respective degree of importance.

Improving Your Social Environment

A quote from fantasy author Kayla Krantz: "When we force something to fit where it doesn't belong, it breaks. When surrounded by people who can't appreciate our beauty, humans essentially do the same."

Similar to a soldier functioning in the enemy (hostile) territory, so too is the unrest and limited capacity of people functioning in deleterious social environments. Nonetheless, the awareness of the (social) situation allows the soldier (individual) to adapt their behaviors accordingly. Although still able to function, performance will be drastically reduced.

A conducive social environment would be one where individual social needs are being met or, at the very least, have the chance to be satisfied. A deleterious social environment would therefore be one where social needs are ignored or left unfulfilled. Individuals should always aim to cultivate and maintain a healthy social environment. If not possible in a particular situation, it would be beneficial to remove oneself from that particular circumstance to function optimally.

Concerning the impact of the social environment, consideration can now be placed on managing the aforementioned three social needs. In doing so, individuals can now position themselves in social settings that allow them to perform at their peak. In addition, it affords the people with this knowledge to impact their environment, if possible, and improve their well-being and performance.

In terms of affection, individuals need to feel taken care of. Not to say that the individual is not fully capable of taking care of themselves and their responsibilities. However, the fact that another individual/entity outside of themselves would willingly invest in their well-being creates a sense of security (real or imagined).

Personal and working relationships last longer and perform better when the individual parties look after each other outside of the required considerations of that relationship. Businesses that take care of their employees, in the form of good salaries and conducive working environments, for example, retain employees for longer and, as a result, boost the efficiency of business operations.

Similarly, intimate relationships form stronger bonds when partners feel like they are considered (loved) in the decision-making and daily happenings within the relationship. A wedding anniversary that is celebrated by only one partner "showing love" every year will undoubtedly face some issues, in comparison to both partners giving adequate consideration.

Regarding behavioral confirmation, individuals should place themselves in situations (personal/work) where they are appreciated and their efforts recognized. This creates a positive affect which helps motivate the individual and related behavior. Conversely, a setting where one's need for affection is not fulfilled produces a negative affect, not to mention decreases productivity.

Among numerous reasons why an individual would seek out status, Barkow pointed out the importance of relative standing for preferential access to resources. High standing is associated with prestige and access as these individuals are considered to have proven their value and contributions given their standing (success). Status is therefore very much related to perceived success [11].

Following the information presented, the degree to which a person emphasizes one social need over another will determine the degree to which they will be affected if the need is left unsatisfied. Nevertheless, each of the three factors contributes to the type and quality of the social environment that a person is exposed to.

Treasure Trove

The environment is a limitless resource of information if we can extract meaning from it and subsequently apply it. In the social context, we gain insight by observing people, actions, outcomes, and feedback from our social interactions/relationships.

If we examine child raising, for example, a child's first social environment is that of the family. This child is constantly observing the dynamics–social and otherwise–

between family members themselves. From these observations, they begin to make assumptions, guidelines, and conclusions about the world around them.

That is why, for example, a child who observes love as material bestowment will emulate that same behavior when expressing love. On the other hand, if the child observes love as care and sacrifice for another, then his action will also follow suit.

Knowledge gained from social experiences can be used to adapt behaviors or adopt/abandon new ones. This phenomenon is called social modeling and can have positive or negative effects. Healthy social relationships are catalysts for personal development and efficient progress while unhealthy social relationships hinder them.

A healthy social environment is not a matter of happenstance, rather, it can be created and maintained from the knowledge and effort of all parties involved. It would therefore be reasonable to assume that individuals have an element of control in creating their social environments. Conversely, there are social elements that impose control on the individual.

The impact of the social environment on an individual is subtle and usually occurs over time. Because of its indirect nature, people tend to underestimate the impact of that social environment on their behavior. Nonetheless, the resulting impact(s) on individual behavior is undebatable.

If your efforts are not appreciated at work, then you don't feel valued or recognized. As a result, you gradually put less effort into your work which decreases your performance output. Decreased performance output means increased scrutiny by management. Increased scrutiny means increased stress and pressure. Increased stress and pressure could lead to health issues that prevent you from working, and the downward spiral continues.

On the other hand, if your work is appreciated or recognized, you put in increased effort to maintain good standing. Increased effort means increased performance output. Increased performance output may lead to acknowledgment by management in the form of a bonus or promotion. A promotion will increase your quality of life and, hopefully, your spirits.

Expose yourself to social relations that fulfill social desires, especially those you hold in high regard. If you work in a place where you feel undervalued, then it would be better to find a job that does. If your friends don't make you feel worthy, then find some that do. Collaborate with people that bring you up, not down.

Observing successful people and their behavior can also provide valuable insight into how you could be successful too. Find people in parallel fields of study/work and analyze their behavior. If they are successful, that means that their behaviors and strategies have already been proven effective.

Action Steps

1. Learn in real life: True learning cannot be achieved in a social vacuum. Individuals are products of their environment. Social context allows for better teaching, understanding, and subsequent use of a concept–the bigger picture.

For example, when learning a foreign language, one is taught the standard way of communicating. In the classroom, students are taught standard pronunciations, vocabulary intonations, and everything else they need to know. After a few months of classroom learning and preparation, you take a trip to a foreign country where the language is spoken. You are excited and feel prepared for your new adventure.

However, when you get there and begin to communicate with the local people, you barely understand anything they say. Strange, right? Actually, no it is not. It is actually pretty common. The local people have their own way of speaking the language based on their history and culture. Therefore, the language becomes less distinguishable than what they had initially learned.

Just as English is spoken in many different countries but they all speak it differently, there are different speeds, accents, vocabulary, etc., that are specific to the region, and provide the social context for the way it is spoken. American English sounds different from British English, and many people have problems understanding one over the other although they are both considered the English language.

2. Prioritize your needs: Needs are not negotiable, yet we tend to bargain and settle when it comes to our psychological and social needs. We need to breathe, and we need to sleep. Deprivation of either will have catastrophic effects on the human body because they are physical needs. They are more observable and verifiable, so naturally, people focus on their maintenance.

Psychological and social needs carry the same risk of damage to the self, but due to their internal and psychological nature, their effects are less observable and quantifiable. Nonetheless, deprivation of social needs causes less easily noticeable effects that negatively impact the individual.

3. Control your environment: Don't let your environment control you. Without cognizant action, we truly are just products of our environment. Surround yourself with people that encourage your development and prioritize your social needs.

The social needs relationship goes both ways. The same way that your social needs must be satisfied, so does the social needs of others. Every individual needs to contribute towards a healthy social environment by providing valuable feedback to those around you, including you.

Sometimes we are the source of the feedback that others use to alter or learn new behaviors. In those moments we need to be able to make a valuable contribution to the group and environment by extension.

If you notice someone struggling due to social pressures or circumstances, offer help and advice. These types of good deeds are often reciprocated and contribute to the healthy social environment that people need.

Find a healthy social environment. If that's not possible, then start building it yourself. Choose the right people to be around you, to learn from, and to support you. Addressing the social issue surrounding your performance will clear the path to achieve your goals.

Key Reader Takeaways

- The status of your social needs impacts your performance. These needs are satisfied based on the quality of your social environment. Choose or build wisely.
- We get quality feedback from the people around us and the way they interact with the world around them. Be observant of your surroundings and extract all valuable information.

6

GPS (GOAL POSITIONING SYSTEM)

The Ocean Tide

> Life is like an ocean. It can be calm and still or rough and rigid, but in the end, it's always beautiful. - Anonymous

Many live their lives striving towards a destination (goal-oriented). They have an idea of what they want their life to be like and then take the necessary actions to achieve it. Some live life more freely and allow the destination to reveal itself with time, while others are powerless to the tides of life and are simply taken along for the ride.

Imagine a ship in the open seas. The open sea is representative of life and its vast potential, while the ship represents an individual as they attempt to navigate it. The course of the ship, and whether or not it arrives at its destination, will be determined by different factors, including the tides, winds, and one's ability to navigate.

Figuratively speaking, the tides represent the uncontrollable nature of life. There are times when life pushes and pulls us in different directions. Sometimes these forces work to our benefit, and at other times to our detriment.

With the advancement of technology, for instance, many assembly-line jobs have been reassigned to automatic machinery. These machines are more precise and efficient than humans, and as a result, many companies have laid much of the human workforce due to redundancy.

The loss of employment was not due to the actions/inactions of the employees but rather a result of circumstances. The fault lies nowhere, yet its effect is potent and far-reaching. In these circumstances (opposing tide), moving forward will prove difficult.

A more fortuitous scenario, like winning the lottery, for example, can open multiple avenues for progress. In an instant, a situation can go from dire and stressful to lavish and composed. It is no secret that money can open doors and allow access to previously inaccessible opportunities. The way forward is only limited by the individual.

Advantageous or disadvantageous circumstances (tides) do not guarantee that the action or route taken will end in success or failure respectively. A fortuitous situation can quickly turn into a grim one, and vice versa, depending on how the individual handles their respective situations.

One cannot affect the tides, but can control their effect on the trajectory of your ship (life). Similar to how a ship captain steers his ship, so too must individuals navigate the particular tides of their lives. Furthermore, an experienced captain knows how to use the tides to their benefit and, when not possible, how to ride out the storm.

The tide signifies external forces outside the individual that will impact his life. These external forces can originate from your living, social or working environments and influence behavior. However, not everyone caught in the same tide will end up at the same location. Individuals under similar circumstances can display completely different behaviors.

Winds Of Ambition

The wind represents our ambitions and our attitudes toward them. The wind can be a great force for propelling a ship in the right direction. In the same way, the absence of wind, or wind from the wrong direction, can make it more difficult to control and ultimately get to where you want to go.

Ambition can be defined as a personal disposition characterized by the persistent and generalized striving for success, attainment, and accomplishment [1]. When we hold positive attitudes about our ambitions, then the strong winds of our belief thrust us into motion making goals feel more attainable and destinations more reachable.

Rather than a single entity, ambition is a collection of psychological characteristics. Barsukova proposed the following grouping of the psychological characteristics of ambition:

1. Goals: Personal/professional goals and plans for achieving them.

2. Self-attitude: Satisfaction and dissatisfaction in oneself and one's achievements.

3. Attitude towards other people: Friend or foe, competitor or ally, threat or harmless?

4. Attitude towards professional activity: Willingness to do more than required on the job (e.g., overtime, or taking the initiative).

5. Self-regulation: Mental and emotional stability, adaptability, and willingness to take risks.

6. Achievement motivation: The desire to win, be successful, and achieve self-actualization.

7. Cognitive characteristics: Critical thinking, open-mindedness, and flexibility [2].

These psychological characteristics of ambition are interconnected and interrelated and contribute to achieving an ambitious state and associated behavior. The primary goal of ambitious people is to be recognized socially as a top performer (or a success) or simply to distinguish themselves from the rest.

Ambition is a powerful influencer in many social contexts as it has a substantial effect on work, career behavior, and outcomes [3], such as job performance [4]. For example, an ambitious disposition can lead to motivational states (e.g., working harder/longer and higher levels of work-related commitment) that drive work-related behaviors and job performance [5].

It is important to note that ambition is not inherently good or bad. Depending on your culture or religion, for example, ambition may be considered a "good" or "bad" personal trait to have. More correctly, it is the resulting action/course of ambition that could be deemed as such.

The dilemma of the "true nature" of ambition becomes a central topic, especially when referring to blind ambition. Blind ambition refers to the relentless pursuit of one's goals with little to no regard for what's happening around you. Individuals may not be aware or are simply unconcerned with how the people and environment are affected by their unyielding pursuit of ambitions.

On one hand, this super-focused state of mind is like adding a motor to your ship. These individuals will certainly get to their destination faster. Usually, their route is shortened by working harder/longer, avoiding stops/useless detours, or taking a more direct (dangerous/difficult) route to their destination. Research results showed that ambition is significantly related to adaptive performance at work [6].

On the other hand, this kind of behavior can lead to negative outcomes since individuals may sacrifice time socially or with family in order to achieve their goals. They are not concerned with the impact of their presence or absence on the lives of the people around them.

Ambition, in itself, is like a powerful motivational engine. Unadulterated ambition can be like a force of nature, though blind ambition is different. With more power, the ability to control direction (navigate) is reduced. Individuals then run the danger of crashing into obstacles and making their journey a more difficult one.

O Captain, My Captain

Navigation is the most crucial aspect of getting to your destination. Being lost at sea is not a pleasant experience, literally or figuratively. However, you will only consider yourself lost when you don't know or recognize where you are.

When we take note of where we are, we can then understand how to get to where we want to go. The first step in navigating is doing just that: determining your location.

Determining one's location (standing) provides the starting point from which one departs in attempting to reach their destination (goal). In doing so, a person can better evaluate the time and effort needed to arrive at the desired destination. Closer destinations feel more attainable and require less effort while further destinations require more effort, time and planning.

For example, a trip to the corner store requires little effort and time. The store is located nearby and you are already familiar with their products and prices. Traveling to another country to shop, on the other hand, would require significantly more effort and planning.

Figuratively speaking, the journey to a far-off island (to become an airline pilot) may be a long one that requires preparation (years of schooling, training, and practice). Whereas the journey to the nearest island on the way (graduate flight school) will require significantly less time and effort. Turning a long tiresome trip into multiple shorter ones makes the entire trip more manageable.

The next step in the navigation process is plotting a course. Individuals that go through life with a positive attitude towards navigating the seas of life tend to achieve their goals and reach their destinations. Often this is because they feel prepared to deal with obstacles and are confident in their ability to navigate the optimal (shortest/safest) route for getting there.

Their positive attitude and ambitions move their ships in the right direction and motivate continued action even in the face of the tides (obstacles). For these individuals, the tides are of little consequence in the face of their ambition.

On the other hand, individuals that possess a negative attitude towards navigating the seas of life seldom achieve their goals or reach their destinations. This is because they may feel unprepared, unable or unwilling to deal with the obstacles they would inevitably encounter.

Their lack of ambition and/or negative attitudes is like still air on a windless day. Their ship is at the whims of the tides, and they fail to exhibit any form of control over the direction of their ship. They are merely passengers on a ride and hope that they can eventually get to their destination or any destination for that matter.

Still, human desires may provide destinations throughout the course of life, but desire alone is insufficient for attaining goals. For example, a managerial position opens up in your company and you have always wanted to be a manager, so you apply for the position. Unfortunately, you don't get the position, and it is awarded to someone else. You fail to understand why you were not selected and become upset and frustrated.

This may not seem like an ideal opportunity, but frustrating situations never do. Nevertheless, taking note of where you are in the scenario can shed some light on why you didn't get the position and what needs to be done to ensure that your goal can still be accomplished in the future.

Fate Or Destiny

In the aforementioned scenario, if the individual had taken note of their standing, they would have realized that they were not the only person applying for the managerial position. Moreover, the other candidates had more experience than them and, most importantly, possessed some kind of managerial degree.

In considering these circumstances, the individual feels less slighted. The company made the best decision in hiring the most qualified applicant, although it may not feel like it to the passed-over individual. By keeping track of where you stand, you can better understand how to maneuver obstacles in your way and what it will take to get to your destination.

For instance, getting one's bearings in the previous situation would be understanding that a managerial role would be unattainable without the necessary degree. Therefore, one possible option could be going to (night) school to finish your degree or earn some form of managerial certification. This will definitely increase your chances of obtaining that new position.

These individuals live their lives according to destiny. They believe that they choose the course of their lives themselves and that destiny is within their control, thus, find ways to shape it themselves. Instead of being a victim of the tides, these individuals choose to navigate a course in order to get to their destination.

Every skilled navigator knows that there is usually more than one way to get to a destination, some more perilous (difficult) than others. A course is plotted in advance to ensure that one is headed in the right direction and provide insight into what is to be expected– bad weather, rough seas, strong tides.

Plotting a course is only possible when you know your current location. Moreover, a route deemed unfit for whatever reason, can be altered to accommodate any obstacles in the way and, at the same time, ensures that you are heading toward your destination (goal). When lost or off course, such individuals reorient themselves using the information around them, for example, the stars, the sun, the moon (i.e. the environment), and can then adjust their direction accordingly.

Other individuals, fail to keep track of their standing and put themselves at a disadvantage. They fail to understand why they are unable to reach their destination (goal), and often, their journeys are forcefully abandoned. No one wants to give up on their goals, but it makes no sense to chase unattainable goals, at least unattainable in one's mind.

These individuals are victims of fate. They feel lost and powerless, with no idea how to get back on the right track. This is because they lack the ambition and attitude to reach their destination; there is no wind in their sails. Instead, they rely on the tides and good fortune when dealing with obstacles, and have no particular route in mind.

Though being a victim of fate doesn't guarantee unfavorable odds or undesirable results, you are simply a passenger on the ship. In the same way, as the captain, choosing your destination doesn't guarantee favor and success.

Ships often navigate the open seas with no land in sight. Ships head in the direction of their destination with faith and the capabilities for getting there. They do not see their destination from the start but firmly believe that they will arrive there in time with the correct heading.

They plot the best route based on their knowledge and experience. Furthermore, if previous ships had successfully taken that route and arrived at their destination safely, then that would be more reason to select or continue on that path. That is not to say that the route selected is without its obstacles, but being aware of these (potential) obstacles makes it easier to navigate.

Action Steps

1. Know yourself: As an engine is to a car and wind is to sail ships, so too is ambition to individual behavior. Ambition can be a useful tool for transporting an individual to where they want to go in life, but not all engines are the same, and not all winds gust.

One of the most undervalued and unappreciated concepts out there is the truth. Often because it is not a pretty sight, hence the term "the ugly truth." Nonetheless, the value of truth is priceless, particularly during self-observation and personal development.

You boast to your friends that you can play the guitar when you know you barely manage to stumble through one song. If your skills were to be put to the test, the results would not be in your favor. Moreover, the fallout of such a dismal performance would have significant impacts on the individual and social environment.

Another person dreams of being a doctor one day, while they have never even taken a free course in health education. Another dreams of becoming the CEO of the company when they have never taken the initiative when given the opportunity.

Individuals need to be honest with themselves and their current state of being to ascertain the starting point alluded to earlier. We possess our goal/desire, but before we commence that journey, we must first find our bearings. Sometimes, the first thing to be done is to admit that you are lost or at the very least, on the wrong route.

Honesty with oneself and one's situation will greatly aid in plotting a course and overcoming obstacles along the way. A captain will not set sail knowing that there is a fierce storm on the horizon (situation), nor will he ship off without adequate rations (skills) less the consequences be dreadful.

Knowing and understanding oneself brings clarity of purpose and enforces ambitious behavior. For example, a professional boxer fighting for sport and another fighting to provide for their family will have different types and levels of ambition. The winner may yet be decided but irrespective of skill, the latter would be a safer bet.

2. Know your environment: "Therefore, to estimate the enemy situation and to calculate distances and the degree of difficulty of the terrain to control victory are the virtues of the superior general" – Sun Tzu

Do you drive the same way in sunny weather as you do in rainy or snowy? Do you act the same way you do at home as you do at work or socially? If you drive more cautiously due to the rainy weather, then you would be better prepared for an abrupt stop. Furthermore, I doubt your manager would appreciate being called Uncle Bill.

Being aware of your environment helps better prepare you for obstacles, foreseen or unexpected, that may arise. When obstacles surpass the ability of the individual, then the route can be adjusted to improve the chances for success. Without the knowledge of the surrounding, navigation would not be possible.

People are innately able to navigate through their social environments through experience and observation however taking note of the unique qualities of every situation (social, working, personal) could aid in determining the safest route for getting to your destination/goal.

Additional information, whether from external or internal sources, can be used to guide individual action. Understanding your ambitions is no different.

<u>3. Choose your destiny</u>: Writer and entrepreneur, Stephen C. Lundid said, "There is always a choice about the way you do your work, even if there is not a choice about the work itself."

A lot of what happens in our lives is a result of our choices. We can decide to be better, work harder or develop ourselves. There will undoubtedly be obstacles along the way no matter what route you choose, but being prepared will assist in overcoming or avoiding obstacles when necessary.

The first and most difficult obstacle in the path of your success is you. Whether intentional or unintentional, the way we think, feel, and understand a situation will determine our attitude, actions, and behavior. Therefore, individuals should build positive attitudes about working towards their goals and use ambitions as a stepping stone for getting to their destination.

<u>Key Reader Takeaways</u>

- Individuals can share destinations (goals) but every journey is different and unique.
- Ambition is a tool, whether the results are favorable or not depends on how it is employed.
- Every journey begins with preparing oneself physically or mentally for what is to come.
- Learn to use your surroundings, internal and external, to navigate through life.

7

IDENTIFY YOUR PURPOSE

T hought can be considered the ground zero of the human experience. The way that people perceive and interpret the world is processed and understood with thought. However, not everyone thinks the same way or at the same level, which results in the limitless variety of the individual human experience (i.e., life).

Just as the host often forgets to include themselves when totaling the number of guests for dinner, so too do people fail to consider themselves as participators and contributors to their life experience. So much focus is placed on ensuring that all observable factors (guests, dinner plates, amount of food) are addressed that self-inclusion is left for last or left out entirely.

An event organizer, for example, plays a central role in the organization and subsequent outcome of an event. Understandably, their ability to plan and execute the desired event would come into question. We are the event organizers of our lives. Therefore, should we not also evaluate ourselves and our abilities to plan and live the life we choose?

Some of us are not qualified for the type of life we want. You want wealth, success, and fame but lack ambition, focus, and a social network. You want to own your own business one day but haven't taken a single business course in your life. You want to get married and settle down, but go on different dates every weekend.

On the bright side, qualifications can be obtained and upgraded to meet the requirements. Individuals can discover their ambitious sides, improve focus, and build their social networks. Entrepreneurs can take classes and join seminars to establish a foundation, and individuals who want to get married can choose quality over quantity of dates.

In addition to the unqualified, some people are just not suited for a certain kind of life while others fit into it like a glove: country life versus city life, loner versus pack, modern versus conventional, lawyer versus artist, etc. People spend most of their lives looking for the place where they fit, and where they belong–their purpose.

Philosophically speaking, our purpose as humans has been debated for millennia, but our individual purposes in life need to be unearthed on our own. One needs to dig deep beneath the surface of themselves in order to discover the true sources of our actions through self-observation.

Purpose provides meaning and significance to one's life and actions. Purpose in life has been linked to a decrease in mortality across all ages. [1] Moreover, research has shown that a purpose in life is associated with increases in health and longevity across cultures, sexes, and age groups. [2]

Having a purpose assists in dealing with psychological problems like anxiety, stress [3], and depression [4]. People with a purpose in life experience conflict less often by employing effective self-regulatory skills, particularly when making health-related decisions resulting in better health outcomes. [5]

A purpose in life impacts not only individual happiness and performance but also the well-being and happiness of people around them [6]. Within the family dynamic, these people will include immediate family members, while with regard to work, they would be colleagues and coworkers.

People come from different cultures, financial backgrounds, and social statuses. Nevertheless, in life, the necessity of having a purpose is always constant. Life can have meaning even in the most impoverished circumstances. [7,8] We all have a place and purpose; we just need to find it.

Specializing

With most careers, specializing in a particular area allows for a deeper understanding of certain subject matter and, as a result, an improved performance. Before becoming a neurosurgeon, for instance, an individual needs to complete several years of general training and education in medicine. After completing the general studies, their medical knowledge and ability broaden but are superficial in many areas.

General study is followed by a period of specialization where doctors learn specific knowledge pertaining to the topic of neuroscience and its application. By specializing in a particular field, doctors clarify their purpose of study and can focus on improvement and mastery.

Adopting a similar approach in clarifying one's abilities, capabilities, and goals can greatly increase your chances of finding your purpose. Clarity of purpose allows us to concentrate focus, efforts and abilities on a particular area or outcome. On the other hand, people who keep searching for meaning without finding it are often dissatisfied with themselves and their relationships [9].

Baumeister and Vohs explain that, most often, purpose must be found, created, or learned [10]. Most people focus their efforts on finding their purpose amongst the myriad of potential possibilities in life. They are not afraid to try new things/situations and use that feedback to determine their state of happiness and well-being.

People who succeed in finding their purpose seem to fit into their lives like a glove. They are content with their work, feel rewarded with their outcomes, and thrive within their environment. Whether it be the result of happenstance or revealed through hard work, they are both qualified and suited for the life they lead.

Creating and learning your purpose on the other hand requires a different kind of consideration due to the uniqueness of one's individual circumstances. Creation implies the birth of a new unique purpose that the individual instigates. Sometimes your purpose doesn't fit into the currently available options. The only way forward from there is to create that position/place/purpose.

Learning your purpose is required when there is insufficient knowledge of oneself or available options. For example, a young talented athlete who focuses his efforts on his studies instead of his passion for and skill in sports. He has been taught that sports are not the avenue for success and accomplishing great things.

As he grows, he learns from the news, the Olympics, and other observable factors, that sports actually could lead to his desired outcomes of success and achievement. He can now combine his passion for sports with his desired goal for success, i.e., purpose. What an individual finds important helps to ignite passion, as it is more values-based and will contribute to self-concordance [11].

Finding the perfect fit (purpose) in life requires a person to know their size (themselves). No amount of willpower can get a size 9 foot into a size 4. Although a size nine could manage to fit into a size 8, it would surely be uncomfortable and, with enough time, unbearable. Instead, research suggests that reflecting on and writing down personal goals is especially important in helping people to find purpose and live a fulfilling life [12].

Unsurprisingly, the information being sought originates from, and is based on, the particular individual. Have you ever tried to buy clothes for someone and, as it turned out, they did not fit them correctly? You are the best person to determine your size and comfortableness in clothes (life).

Finding our purpose begins with finding, understanding, and developing ourselves. Only in this way does one have a chance of flourishing along the path they were destined for.

Self-Esteem Vs. Self-Doubt

The way one perceives themselves, their ability and potential will determine the likelihood of success or achievement of their goal/purpose. If you see yourself as a success, then you will be successful. If you see yourself as a failure, then you will inevitably fail.

Confidence and self-doubt can affect performance in different ways, some less obvious than others. For instance, a student who has studied and prepared for an exam should behave differently from those who have not.

With one look around the class, one can easily distinguish the confident ones from the nervous ones. Confidence and nervousness are external representations of the internal mental state. Therefore, it would be reasonable to assume that the confident students perform better than the nervous ones.

The ones who studied now possess the relevant information to pass the test. This is verifiable by their often calm and collected demeanor. They believe that they will pass the test and come out of the situation on top. On the other hand, those who did not study lack the vital information and have little faith in their ability to succeed. They are now concerned and frantic.

Uncertainty about one's ability in performance may suggest the possibility of failure and elicit protective behaviors as a defense mechanism. Self-handicapping is a prime example of this kind of protective behavior [13].

Research from Jones and Berglas found self-handicapping to be a mechanism used to protect the individual's self-esteem by attributing possible failure to external causes rather than their clear lack of ability. Basically, these individuals look for excuses for their (poor) performance [14].

For example, an employee who is passed over for a promotion opportunity may claim favoritism before they accept that they are less qualified than the competition.

Further still, some employees will not even apply for the position for fear of winning the position and performing poorly. Although this methodology protects the individual's self-image, it undermines the validity and assessment of their performance.

Overachieving is another good example of protective behavior. Overachieving, an opposite strategy to self-handicapping, was found to be used by individuals who both doubted their abilities and had strong concerns about performing successfully [15].

True confidence comes from acknowledgment. Acknowledging that one knows and understands the subject matter. In the same way, acknowledging that one does not know or understand the subject matter. The latter may be counterintuitive but valid, nonetheless.

Confidence is based on the honest assessment of the individual's capacities and ability to reach their goal. For instance, the student who has taken numerous practice tests and passed every one with flying colors is duly confident in their ability.

On the other hand, a student who has failed every practice test doubts their ability to perform. Nonetheless, they are aware of their inadequate level and can increase their level of effort to ensure success [16]. As a result of their increased effort, performance will also improve, proving, surprisingly enough, that a little self-doubt can increase your performance.

A false sense of confidence is created when individuals base their self-belief on unsupported assumptions and unverifiable information. They also possess supreme confidence in their ability, however unfounded. Having a false sense of confidence can work against you if/when the individuals come to the quick realization that they were not as prepared as they thought they were.

A false sense of confidence doesn't necessarily mean that the individual lacks the information or skills to achieve a goal. It simply means that their skills have not been fully acknowledged and verified by themselves. In the same way, nervous or frantic behavior doesn't always denote incapability or lack of information, but more of a failure to acknowledge/verify them.

A fully prepared straight-A student can look very frantic before an exam. You've practiced for an interview for months, yet, on the day of the interview, you cannot say a word. Some can overcome their nerves and land the job, while others cannot.

The issue at hand is the disconnect between perceived ability and self-confidence. The verification of abilities forms the connective bridge that allows confidence to rise and fall accordingly. Reviewing past successful exams or engaging in practice interviews are good ways of strengthening the connection beforehand.

Positive affirmations are also an excellent way to build one's confidence. Remind yourself that you are intelligent and hard-working. Encourage yourself to be the best version of yourself. It is always good to reward and acknowledge your past and current accomplishments.

Belief in oneself, whether true or unverified, is a way to display to the outside world your knowledge and skill in that particular area. It is an observable expression of the internal status of the individual pertaining to a subject or behavior. Hence, society will assume that confident persons possess all the necessary traits and information for their success, thus their demeanor. On the other hand, frantic or sporadic behavior is seen as the result of being unprepared or unqualified.

Some individuals have a sense of confidence that is warranted, while for others, it may be unwarranted. Nonetheless, in the eyes of society, confidence is equivalent to competence and therefore success. True confidence cannot be validated if no doubt exists to instigate the verification process.

Taking Responsibility

How can one discover their natural talent to paint when they've never picked up a paintbrush? How will you improve your leadership skills when you shy away from responsibilities?

One of the most common reasons why people struggle to find their purpose is fear–fear of the unknown, of being different, of failing–and the list goes on. Furthermore, individuals may feel unqualified or unable to handle certain tasks due to a false sense of self and negative attitudes.

"I can't be the general manager. I've never had that position before." "I'll never get that promotion. There are just too many qualified applicants." "I can't raise two kids on my own. I don't know how to." Negative thoughts and perceptions of oneself prevent people from discovering or building up their true selves.

If you already think that you cannot do something, then you can't do it. Actions and behaviors begin with thought, so before action is taken, thought occurs. The mind leads and the body follows, so if you think or believe you can do it, then you can.

These feelings of ability or inability originate from the metacognitive experience and help guide our actions. However, sometimes these feelings are not based on factual information but rather on our minds' perception of our ability. Our actual capabilities and what our mind assumes are one's capabilities can be two different things.

A purpose is different from *the* purpose. A hammer can be used to break a window but it can also be used to build a house. The true purpose of the hammer is to build, although destruction is another purpose it could be used for. I doubt the hammer would have any preference for the outcome since it is simply a tool. The user, on the other hand, would have had to plan and execute, therefore would have had the desired outcome.

A builder's purpose is to build. When tasked outside of their purpose, fishing for example, then their effectiveness in their role will certainly be diminished. Sometimes, the builder will be forced into fishing as a means of survival and providing for their families. With time these builders will become better fishermen, but from a certain perspective, their talents are wasted in fishing.

Furthermore, true builders by nature may become discontented with their lives as fishermen and, as a result, impact their lives negatively. Feelings of unhappiness and unsatisfied desires plague their minds and affect their behavior even when knowing full well the lack of a better option.

Your purpose could involve taking care of your family, affecting your community or career choice. It is one of the most important factors that guide human behavior and decision-making. It is also a significant contributor to mental health and general well-being.

Life is not as straightforward as people may hope. "Here is your purpose. Now go fulfill it," is not something that you would expect to hear. Moreover, with the vast possibilities out there, finding a purpose may seem intimidating at first, but with time and the right skill set, practically anything is possible.

Action Steps

1. Watch your thought: The mind is a powerful tool that needs to be directed and focused on ensuring precision

and effectiveness. It's easy to get carried away by thought, voluntarily through high levels of focus (e.g., tunnel vision) and low levels (e.g., daydreaming).

Thought shapes your reality and can be a great asset when determining one's purpose. Think about what you want. What makes you happy? What makes you tick? What drives you? What are you passionate about?

Self-discovery begins with thought and analysis. If you like the way you think, then develop it. If you don't then adapt it to your needs. The process may be an easy or short one, but it begins with the right way to think about the world and about oneself.

2. Evaluate yourself and situation: You are the most important contributor to finding your purpose, so you need to be qualified to do so. Look for your strengths, understand them, then master them. Look for your weaknesses, improve upon them or replace them. Change is inevitable with growth.

Search for and expect to find areas that require attention and possible change. Imagine, for instance, that you are responsible for correcting your own test paper and assigning the grade. As you go through your finished paper, you discover errors and problems with some of your answers.

It would be very tempting, and even easier, to "adjust" some of the errors and improve your final grade. However, that would not be a true reflection of your abilities. Although your performance was an A based on the assessment, your true grade was a C. With a C grade, there is room for improvement while there is no perceivable improvement to be made on an A.

3. Gain qualification: The settling thing about qualifications is that they can be earned or obtained. They are attainable goals that can be achieved through time and effort. However, to gain qualification is to admit that one is unqualified, to begin with.

It is not human nature to readily accept negative or disadvantageous things about oneself. Nobody likes to hear that they are ignorant or inefficient, but the truth of the matter is that some people just are. Nevertheless, these are not permanent circumstances and can be overcome when the individual is ready.

Overqualification is rarely an issue for finding a job or purpose. The issue commonly arises in the payment or reward for the aforementioned job. No company is not going to hire you because you would fit too well or be too effective. Gain as much experience and qualifications pertaining to your field of study/work.

4. Specialize: We can never know all, but we can know some. We cannot do everything but we can do some things. Identifying our purpose can often coincide with our natural strengths or tendencies. When we discover them, we should improve and sharpen our abilities to increase our chances of success. You may not be able to do the backstroke or breaststroke, but given the right

opportunity, you could doggy paddle across an entire lake.

5. Believe in yourself: Some individuals may take their self-confidence for granted, but belief in yourself is vital for achieving any goal. Sometimes, confidence is well-founded, and other times, it is flimsy as a twig. Build up belief in yourself and abilities with research and practice, knowledge and experience.

Belief in oneself is seen as confidence by others. Confidence in oneself then inspires the same belief in others. Someone who is unskilled but confident has a better chance of success than someone who is skilled but has extreme self-doubt. Moreover, a confident person will be deemed more qualified, and potentially more successful, than someone who is not. Belief is infectious but it begins with believing in oneself.

6. Verify: Experience is often referred to as the greatest teacher. Expose yourself to situations and people that build up your confidence and instigate personal development. Most of all, use these circumstances to verify your ability and purpose.

It is important that the individual is honest with themselves and the results of their verification. It is only in the acceptance of the results that one can begin to make changes for the better. At this point, one takes note of their standing and determines whether or not their confidence is warranted.

Positive verification leads to increased confidence and performance. Negative verification can also lead to improved performance by way of increased effort.

Key Reader Takeaways

- You are what you think you are. If you see yourself as an entrepreneur, then you act like an entrepreneur and be seen as one as well. It all begins with you.
- You are only limited by your thought.
- Internal feedback (from yourself) is just as important as external feedback (from others).
- It's okay if you don't always believe in yourself sometimes. A little self-doubt can keep you on your toes.
- When in doubt, verify. Evidence is the only way to confirm or deny or to prove innocent or guilty. When there is overwhelming evidence in any case, it's open and shut. Only then will we court know how to proceed.

8

WHAT TO DO WITH SETBACKS AND FEEDBACK

Computers, and many other forms of technology, are now heavily integrated into our lives. Furthermore, they are constantly being updated with software that improves the overall user experience. Take the operating system (OS) of a computer for example. Every so often, a more advanced version of the OS is released with added capabilities and functions.

If you are familiar with using a new OS, you understand that it is never at its optimal performance when just released. This is because the OS was developed in isolation from actual user interaction and therefore must now go through a debugging process as it will be used to carry out different functions by different users.

Developers create an OS under a plethora of varying conditions and possible uses. Nonetheless, inevitably, with time and increased usage of the OS, users discover problems that need to be addressed. An OS will run into errors based on never before processed tasks or overwhelming workloads.

These errors are sent back to the developers who use the information from the failed processes to build or adapt system infrastructure that can properly support and handle that process, and similar ones, in the future. The entire process is repeated with each new error until all, or as many as possible, of the errors are addressed.

The resulting OS, after the debugging process, is much more effective and capable than its predecessor granting users more features and functions when using their computers. Debugging is not dissimilar to the refining process of precious stones, metals, and raw materials. The results of the process are a purer and richer form of its precursor.

Thought can be equated to the OS of our beings while the individual can be considered the developer. Similar to computer development, people's OS (way of thinking) must go through a debugging process to improve one's ability for thought.

Debugging can only be done through user interaction via error reporting and feedback. Without reporting this information, developers are left unaware of the error ultimately ensuring its reoccurrence in the future. Error reporting and feedback are vital to the development, maintenance, and upgrading of any system.

A person's thought (OS) is debugged through their interaction with their internal and external environments. Knowledge equips us with the ability to process varying circumstances and achieve the desired goal. Therefore, the more knowledge, or the bigger the database, the more equipped the OS for handling more difficult processes.

Imagine using a computer from the '90s versus using a computer made in 2022. Fundamentally, they are the same thing, but the computer from 2022 is the result of decades of improvement made on the 90's models and subsequent models thereafter. Aside from its vintage allure, there isn't much reason to use outdated technology or software.

As we live our lives, we run into setbacks (errors) with our thought processes. These setbacks can stem from varying origins like an inadequate database (knowledge), limited processing capacity (metacognition), and communication errors: internal and external devices. Unless these errors are addressed, an OS cannot be upgraded and is doomed to obsolescence.

As the developer of our thought, we need to also understand that our thinking should constantly be undergoing the process of debugging. Developers expect and value the importance of user feedback during the development process. They use user feedback as stepping stones for building a more stable system.

The advantages of an updated device or OS far outweigh those of its original form. For instance, running multiple processes on a slow outdated OS is like waiting for paint to dry. Furthermore, trying to run a single program (thought) could even prove overwhelming, depending on the magnitude of the task.

With any worthwhile endeavor, there will be setbacks. However, the difference between PC developers and developers of thought (regular people) is that they are motivated, financially or otherwise, to create the best OS possible. To do that, they use all the resources at their disposal, and that includes feedback (positive or negative) and setbacks from user interactions.

Windows "Me"

Nowadays, people don't want to wait three seconds for a webpage to load or an app to run. The moment users are unsatisfied with the processing ability of their OS or device, they exchange it for an upgraded version. To avoid this quick overturn in devices, software companies send out regular updates for their software to maintain optimal performance.

Individuals need to motivate themselves by appreciating the value of improved thought. Motivation can be found from within (in the form of personal development or even rewarding feelings) or from without (like financial gain and status). Motivate yourself to improve your thinking as a means of improving your life.

Progressive thinking is the only way to maintain and develop thought to meet the requirements of the times.

Individuals that cannot assimilate and upgrade their way of thought will quickly be left behind with all the other outdated technology. Try asking a teenager what a Walkman is.

As one gains knowledge and experience, one should update/upgrade their way of thinking. That is not to say that conventional patterns of thought do not have fundamental roles in our lives, but they are limited in their application.

For example, the prehistoric notion that women should be housewives and caretakers while men considered the breadwinners. This way of thinking was a reflection of the times since employment at the time usually involved hard labor or functioning in a male-dominated society. Furthermore, women were thought to be better suited (physically, emotionally, or biologically) to child-rearing and managing home affairs.

This way of thinking cannot exist in modern times since society is more knowledgeable and developed than before. In addition, there are more equal opportunities for women and they have proven themselves to be just as capable, if not more so, than men in the working/business world.

Men in powerful positions will fail to see a woman, a rising star, in the company as a threat to their position. Acting per their beliefs and thoughts, they pay little attention to the woman's achievements and personal drive. Her efforts are eventually recognized and appreciated, and with time, she takes the place of the man previously in that powerful position.

His way of thinking was his fatal flaw. If he had seen her as a worthy adversary/competitor, then he would've taken the necessary action to secure his position. Outdated concepts, ideologies, and beliefs can be detrimental to the development of one's thinking. Conversely, updated beliefs and progressive thinking catalyze the growth and development of effective thinking habits.

Progressive thinking is a way to make the impossible possible and the unseen seen. It is like sending regular updates to your OS to prevent recurring errors and issues with processing information. Thought can be improved naturally with experience, with the acquisition of new knowledge, and by seeking out feedback.

The best technologies make life easier or attempt to solve a particular issue. Thought, and its resulting ideas, are similar to technology in that regard. After using a useful tool for long enough, you can no longer imagine life without it, or why you didn't always have/use it, to begin with. Thinking should be goal-oriented and feedback from one's environment provides the direction in which one should focus their efforts.

Computers are the perfect example of how productive technology can be integrated into various aspects of our lives. The computer is so heavily integrated into our lives that people barely remember life without them. They are in our phones, in our homes, and even in our bodies.

What makes PCs so valuable is their programmable and upgradeable nature. The OS can be specially catered to function and behave in certain ways that are beneficial to the overall processing of information and its subsequent result or action. The computer in a car is very different from that of a security system.

Thinking big doesn't always equate to grandiose ideas and lofty goals. Sometimes thinking big could be as simple as providing a new or alternative solution to a problem. For example, in a small accounting firm, an employee suggests changing the filing system from paper to digital form. In effect, this increases the efficiency of the entire company by streamlining its data processing tasks.

Action Steps

1. Be upgradeable: Don't you hate it when you are stuck with a plan or situation when you know that there is a better option out there? The most popular effective products are upgradeable. They take into consideration the quickly developing times and allow room for adaptations in the future.

Products that cannot be upgraded, will quickly be disregarded because of decreased functionality. You don't still see people walking around with pagers on their belts, or people stopping to use a phone booth to connect with friends.

Similar to computers and their OS, regularly check for updates to your thinking. As developers, test out your thinking before you give a user access and things begin to go wrong. Expect things to go wrong (errors) and use that information to upgrade your system and make it more secure.

<u>2. Switch up your routine</u>: Instead of taking the regular route back home, sometimes try a different one. Instead of having your prepared in the usual way, try some new or different types. It's from these new experiences that we can gain additional information about life and ourselves.

<u>Key Reader Takeaways</u>

- Thought is a lifelong upgradeable process.
- As developers of thought, take time to analyze feedback in hopes of streamlining the entire system (way of thought).

9

IMPROVING YOUR FOCUS

Sports are one of the most popular and widely viewed events around the world. From basketball and football to tennis and hockey, millions watch professional players compete against each other. Not every athlete is cut out to be a professional and only some make it to the grand Olympic stage. Nonetheless, anyone with hopes of becoming a skilled professional and possibly an Olympian should train like one as well.

In preparation for the Olympics, an athlete will train for years and sometimes their entire young lives. This speaks to the level of focus (commitment and perseverance) that these athletes possess. As a result of their superhuman efforts, their performance is incomparable to that of the average athlete in a similar field.

One of the most well-renowned athletes of all time is Michael Phelps. For the people who do not know of him, he is a competitive swimmer in a class of his own. In the

2008 Beijing Olympics, Michael Phelps dominated the competition winning eight gold medals. He not only won but broke seven world records in the process.

According to his lifelong coach Bob Bowman, in preparation for the Olympics, Michael had not missed a single day of training in six years. Moreover, his training regimen was incredibly strict with at least two and a half hours of uninterrupted swimming allowing him to cover 10,000m a day. To support his exceptional efforts, Phelps would consume at least 8,000 calories per day.

In a recent study, researchers reveal that, globally, the average distance a person will travel per day is about 5,000 steps or 3,800m [1]. Putting this into proper perspective, this would mean that Michael Phelps would travel at least twice as much as the average person would on foot during swim training alone and in addition to whatever activities and responsibilities he might have had. As a result, his energy and endurance levels are almost scary.

There are times, in training and competition when some athletes experience such an extreme focus on their task that their action, awareness, and control merge seamlessly producing one of their best performances. Every athlete has experienced or at least is aware of the concept of being in the zone or "flow."

In The Zone

Flow is defined as the intense experiential involvement in a moment-to-moment activity, which can be physical or mental [1]. Attention is fully concentrated on the task at hand and the person functions optimally. Although flow is more observable in its physical manifestation, a mental flow is just as potent in producing favorable results.

Imagine using a magnifying glass (focus) and sunlight (effort) to burn a hole through a sheet of paper. When all the rays are focused on one point by the magnifying glass, the light now becomes an overwhelming force. Finding the right placement for the magnifying glass is crucial: too far or too close to the paper, and the rays fail to find a focal point (goal/purpose/desire).

A flow state is achieved when there is: (1) a merging of action and awareness, (2) a sense of control, (3) a transformation of time, and (4) an autotelic experience [2]. Attentional resources are so invested in the task at hand that there are none left over to monitor concepts like duration of time or negative feelings. As a result, the experience is more productive and enjoyable.

According to Csikszentmihalyi, there are key conditions that promote the flow experience including:

1. Clear goals and immediate feedback: Goals help to orientate the person while feedback gives information on goal attainability like distance, effort, pace, etc. [3]

2. A balance of challenge versus skills: Reaching and maintaining positioning within the flow channel requires a delicate balance between our skills and challenges level, otherwise, individuals might experience boredom [4] or apathy [5].

3. An autotelic personality: An autotelic personality is characterized by both receptive qualities like openness to new experiences or a general curiosity in life and active qualities like a tendency to engage in challenging activities and persistence. They also possess an ability to be motivated by intrinsic rewards [6].

In a separate review, researchers listed ten factors that could affect (positively or negatively) the achievement of a flow state: (1) focus, (2) preparation, (3) motivation, (4) arousal, (5) thoughts and emotions, (6) confidence, (7) environmental and situational conditions, (8) feedback, (9) performance and (10) team play and interaction [7]. To some extent, all of these factors have been addressed within the varying chapters of this book.

The Mental Athlete

Michael Phelps dreamt of outmatching the achievements of his compatriot and swimmer Mark Spitz, who won seven gold medals in Munich in the 1972 Olympic Games. In addition, Ian Thorpe, an Australian three-time gold medalist and an early role model for Phelps thought that he couldn't do it.

Michael now possessed the goal, desire, and motivation to make his dream a reality. The only thing missing was acquiring the level of skill that would allow him to achieve his goal, but he was properly motivated to see it through.

Similar to the magnifying glass example earlier, there needs to be a balance between our skills and challenge level. Not all challenges faced by the individual need to be accepted, while others may not be possible to overcome at the moment due to various contributing factors. Selecting achievable goals ensures the motivation and probability of success.

Another useful method for improving focus is strategic laziness. As the term implies, it involves evaluating and selecting situations that the individual deems are justified to work on, either themselves or by another more suitable candidate e.g., the leader. For instance, a manager designating tasks, whenever possible, to more suitable individuals not only guarantees the quality of the product but frees up some of their focus to be applied elsewhere.

As for Michael's case, he chose to focus most of his time and effort on swimming and improving his skills. The more focus he placed on his training, the less focus that was available for other activities (social or personal). Besides, not many people would be able to go about their regular day after such intense daily training sessions.

In preparation for the 2008 Olympic games, Michael Phelps not only established an achievable goal, but he was also intrinsically motivated in that he had a point to prove to himself, Ian Thorpe, and the rest of the world. These factors contributed greatly to Michael achieving a focal point, where all his efforts could be concentrated on winning as many gold medals as possible.

As a result of his superhuman focus, his ability to achieve and maintain a flow state when swimming was like no other. This is what allowed him to reap the fruits of his labor, winning eight gold medals in Beijing proving all the doubters wrong and granting him the most rewarding feeling and experience in achieving his goal.

Even with his unique ability to swim, those eight medals were not all so easily obtained. One of the most memorable of his races was the 100m butterfly. Initially, Phelps was not doing well and was as far back as seventh place. After the turn, miraculously, Phelps attained and maintained a level of flow that astounded even the greatest swimmers.

Phelps managed to come from seventh place to eventually win the race by the slightest of margins: one one-hundredth of a second. The improved focus could be the slight or massive edge needed in achieving your goals through improved thought.

Action Steps

1. Create a focal point: Light concentrated on a single point is significantly more powerful than dispersed light. Even on the brightest of days (with the greatest of efforts),

finding the focal point will prove impossible unless the individual is willing to make adjustments to the magnifying glass (focus).

A better magnifying glass (improved focus) may indeed increase the power/concentration of the rays (efforts) and eventually even without a focal point the paper may begin to burn, however, things are rarely as straightforward. The fact remains, finding the focal point would have been far more efficient and, in addition, allowed the individual to penetrate more than just paper.

Creating a focal point is not as simple as having a goal. Everyone has goals, but not everyone achieves them. A focal point can only be achieved when goals are attained and supplemented by the skills, motivation, and adaptability of the individual.

Ask yourself, how much do you want that promotion at work? Are you willing to sacrifice your free time and invest in your personal improvement? Are you using your environment to your advantage or are you a victim to it?

What would winning that scholarship mean to you? Do you believe that you have done more than the other applicants? What skills or traits differentiate you from the rest?

Turn the embers of your motivation into the flames of your progress. Equip yourself with the mental tools for forging your path and be willing to make the necessary adjustments along the way.

2. Balancing the flow state: Getting married is easy; it's maintaining a marriage that's the hard part. Similarly, achieving a flow state is a difficult task on its own but maintaining the flow state is a separate task altogether. It requires a different type of effort. Furthermore, the goal is not in the establishment of the concept, but the reason for doing so in the first place and maintaining it.

The purpose of marriage is not for the title, but rather, it attempts to maintain a state of "happiness" that is experienced between the individual parties. A married couple may understand better the difference in maintaining that state of happiness for an extended period. Furthermore, a marriage is never a constant state of happiness as circumstances change as life progresses.

People who want their marriages to last understand even though their relationship functions optimally when in that state, they will not always be happy. At times there will be disappointment, disapproval, and sometimes even disloyalty, each bringing its effects. Nonetheless, if they value and focus their happiness over other effects, then any threat to their relationship can be overcome.

Point being, values may differ based on each individual, but remembering what you value maintains and keeps our flow states balanced.

Key Reader Takeaways

- When you truly decide that you want something, the mind and body are willing to achieve it.

However, willingness to achieve doesn't guarantee success. It is now up to the individual to set their limitations and apply a directed effort towards their goal.

- Achieving a flow state begins with your individual predisposition for change. Being able to cut out distractions and channeling your motivation greatly assist in achieving and maintaining flow.
- Motivation can come from both positive and negative sources. Doubt and uncertainty from others can be a crippling experience or a character-building one. Use all types of experiences to fuel yourself.

10

TAKING INITIATIVE

Have you ever received a present on your birthday? How about presents during the Christmas season? Has your significant other showered you with gifts for Valentine's Day? Have you been rewarded for graduating from high school/university? More than likely, your answer to one of those questions is yes.

Few things feel better than being considered and appreciated. It's difficult to imagine someone angrily opening a gift that they have received. Moreover, if the gift were a considerate one, it would further accomplish its purpose of showing gratitude for the person and their efforts.

The tricky thing about the aforementioned occasions is that gift-giving becomes an expected occurrence. Not to say that the gift would not be appreciated regardless of its expected nature. In the same way, if a person doesn't receive a gift at that time, then they become disappointed and upset.

On the other hand, what if your romantic partner showed you appreciation and gave you a gift just because it was Tuesday? If your boss gave you a mini-bonus every time you completed a successful transaction? How would you feel then?

The latter scenarios would have a much more positive effect on the receiving party. That is because the act was not done with an underlying tone of duty or responsibility but solely in consideration and appreciation of the individual. It is difficult not to be further moved by such a pure act.

Taking the initiative involves being the first to begin a task or plan of action. Moreover, it is not a reactive process in that it is not in response to environmental feedback but more a product of intrinsic motivation. There is no obligation for action, yet there are obvious benefits if said action is taken.

Gift giving is not about the actual gift per se, but about showing appreciation of an individual. The gift itself is only the means for achieving that. The best gifts are those that are thoughtful and considerate.

Staying late to complete the report is not just about making the deadline, but proving to yourself and others that you can work well under pressure and display leadership traits. In a way, you can consider staying late to complete the report as a thoughtful and considerate gift to your future self.

The benefit of an action, apparent or not, has to be first recognized as an opportunity before it can be taken advantage of. When an individual deems an action to be beneficial to them, they are more likely to entertain it. If a food is good for their health, then they will more likely consider adding it to their diet, but its addition is not guaranteed.

For example, many people are aware of the benefits of certain foods in their diet, yet they still choose not to eat them for personal reasons. The benefits of exercise are well known, yet you still find people who struggle to get off the couch. There is insufficient motivation to instigate any action.

Often it is because individuals fail to recognize the added value of taking the action. They assess the situation by its superficial nature and associated benefits that by themselves may be inadequate to instigate action.

Individuals that take the initiative tend to recognize the added value or indirect benefits of the action. The greater the benefits that can be recognized from undertaking the action, the more likely it is to occur. Furthermore, if these benefits promote intrinsic motivation, then its chances of occurring increase even further.

Healthy dieting, for example, is difficult for many people to maintain. One of the most common reasons for dieting is weight loss and this is the main reason why many people even consider it. Those who take action based on this superficial reasoning will find it difficult to maintain if they even decide to do it in the first place.

Individuals that succeed in dieting realize that dieting has both direct and indirect benefits for them. Dieting promotes a healthier body, physically and mentally. A healthier body means that you look better, so you have more self-confidence. You feel better, so you're in a better state of mind. And you do better, because your body is functioning optimally. Your mood is also improved and you have more energy throughout the day.

Organized Thought

Human behavior is goal-oriented so there is always a reason behind action. The important thing here is determining which actions are worth being taken and which are not. This is where organized thought plays a critical role. Organized thought allows us to process and deal with information in a more efficient manner.

Training and testing are the best ways to develop organized thought. The results of which are based more on experiential knowledge and therefore form better quality schemata. Stronger foundations (schema) form sturdier structures (thought processes).

Imagine trying to find one location in a city full of disorganized streets and buildings. Navigating the area would prove exceedingly and unnecessarily difficult. Understandably, abandoning the search entirely would be a viable outcome in that sort of scenario. By the time the location is found, individuals may wonder if the journey was even worth all the effort.

On the contrary, finding a location in a well-organized city would be much easier and require significantly less effort. So much so that you could even visit other locations with the time and effort saved on pinpointing the place of interest. Organized thought is similar in that regard as it makes the thinking process easier and more efficient.

The world is full of opportunity and potential for growth. The first step is recognizing these opportunities as such when the time arrives. Get in the habit of thinking critically about every possible decision or action. This will train your mind to see past superficial benefits and see a more total picture of both the direct and indirect implications of a decision.

Action Steps

<u>Create and take opportunities</u>: Taking the initiative can create opportunities for personal and career development in the future. For example, taking up some of the responsibilities of your absentee boss for the day can create opportunities for you down the line.

There is no increase in pay but an increase in the number of working hours and workload. One obvious reason for taking the initiative in this situation is to be in good graces with your boss, maybe. By itself, that may not be enough reason to overcome the apparent disadvantages.

However, by recognizing this as an opportunity to showcase your skill and ability, or a chance to learn valuable skills and experience in a job that you may one day want/have, then the individual would be more likely to take up the initiative. This kind of thinking is what separates the greats from the not-so-great.

Key Reader Takeaways

- First come, first served: Don't wait until an opportunity presents itself, create it. Not later, but now. When an opportunity does present itself, do not hesitate to take advantage. See all situations and potential opportunities for progress, so when deciding to act, the focus is more on the magnitude/significance/number of the benefits rather than determining its validity of opportuneness.

AFTERWORD

The One World Trade Center in New York is the tallest building in the US with a height of 546m to the tip, while in China, The Shanghai Tower is the tallest building in the country reaching 632m high. The tallest building in the world can be found in Dubai as the Burj Khalifa towers over even the tallest of structures with a height of a whopping 828m.

Each of these buildings is considered a superstructure, not only for its sheer height but for the level of planning and engineering required to accomplish such feats. One has no choice but to appreciate the finished structures in all their glory, but what is unseen is even more impressive than what is above the surface.

Before any infrastructure can be established, the most crucial part is to build an adequate foundation to support the building. If the foundation is weak, then the entire infrastructure will be at risk of crumbling. When superstructures are being built, engineers and developers take extra care in first establishing the "super foundation."

The foundations of the One World Trade Center and the Shanghai Tower are both about 30m below surface level while the foundation of the Burj Khalifa is more than 50m deep.

One cannot simply decide to build a superstructure at a given location. The location must be assessed and prepared even before any foundation can be built. Then the necessary steps can be taken to ensure its completion. The same reasoning can be applied to thought and its associated mental infrastructure.

According to Warren Buffet, one of his greatest investments as a youth was purchasing a book called *The Intelligent Investor* [1]. Although he already had a grasp on trading and investing, he was always hungry for more information.

By purchasing the book, Mr. Buffet actually invested in himself, in his thinking. This new information, his metacognitive skills, and his adaptability allowed him to develop and maintain his thought from the ground up and make any necessary changes along the way.

Learning how to think bigger must first be preceded by learning how to think. As intellectual beings, we may take our ability to think for granted. We automatically gain knowledge and experience as we live our lives, but much of this process is widely inefficient in the way that thought is used.

Moreover, our natural capability for thought will differ from individual to individual, as well as our biological or environmental background. Genetics is undoubtedly a contributing factor to mental capacity and hence thought as well. On the other hand, the environment molds us and our thinking as a direct and indirect result.

Out of the many contributors to individual thought, there are those within our control and those that although we cannot control, we can control the effect that the environment has on the development of one's thought processes. The main focus should be on the controllable contributors and aspects and using them to one's advantage.

Building any worthy infrastructure takes time and significant cost. You would not commence building infrastructure without being able to afford it. One needs to gather the necessary investments to ensure that the structure being built is not only completed but of high quality.

Investing in quality materials (metacognition), seeking help from qualified and experienced professionals, colleagues and loved ones (learning and adaptation), and having a motivated workforce (internal and external motivators)are crucial for ensuring success (achievable goals).

Time to take charge as the architect of your thinking.

THE TEAM BEHIND WISDOM UNIVERSITY

Michael Meisner, Founder and CEO

When Michael got into publishing books on Amazon, he found that his favorite topic - the thinking process and its results, is tackled in a much too complex and unengaging way. Thus, he set himself up to make his ideal a reality: books that are informative, entertaining, and can help people achieve success by thinking things through.

This ideal became his passion and profession. He built a team of like-minded people and is in charge of the strategic part and brand orientation, as he continues to improve and extend his business.

Claire M. Umali, Publishing Manager

Crafting books is collaborative work, and keeping everyone on the same page is an essential task. Claire oversees all the stages of this collaboration, from researching to outlining and from writing to editing. In her free time, she writes reviews online and likes to bother her cats.

Kevaughn Francis, Writer

Kevaughn is a passionate writer and language specialist. He has been a teacher for most of his life and uses his background in psychology and varied cultural experiences to cater information to readers, making it more digestible and enjoyable. Kevaughn discovered his talent for language and communication at a young age and continues to foster it to this day.

Alfonso E. Padilla, Content Editor

Mexican editor with a background in journalism. Alfonso takes pride in his curiosity and cares deeply about learning. True to his formation, he prioritizes solid research and sources when reviewing texts. His main tool for editing is the use of questions.

Sandra Agarrat, Language Editor

Sandra Wall Agarrat is an experienced freelance academic editor/proofreader, writer, and researcher. Sandra holds graduate degrees in Public Policy and International Relations. Her portfolio of projects includes books, dissertations, theses, scholarly articles, and grant proposals.

Michelle Olarte, Researcher

Michelle conducts extensive research and constructs thorough outlines that substantiate Thinknetic's book structure. She graduated from Communication Studies with high honors. Her works include screenplays, book editing, book advertisements, and magazine articles.

Ralph Escarda, Layout Designer

Ralph's love for books prevails in his artistic preoccupations. He is an avid reader of non-fictional books and an advocate of self-improvement through education. He dedicates his spare time to doing portraits and sports.

Josie Laica Oronos, Layout Designer

Josie Laica Oronos is a licensed teacher and teaches English to foreign language learners. Josie also loves to spend time with her dogs and cat.

REFERENCES

1. You And Your Thinking

1. Nisbett, R. F., & Ross, I. (1980). *Human inference: Strategies and shortcomings of social judgement.* Englewood Cliffs: NJ: Prentice-Hall.
2. Tversky, A., & Kahneman, D. (1974). Judgment under uncertainty: Heuristics and biases. *Science, 185*, 1124-1131. https://doi.org/10.1126/science.185.4157.1124
3. Wason, P. C. (1966). Reasoning. In B. M. Foss (Ed.), *New horizons in psychology I.* Harmondsworth: Penguin.
4. Ruthsatz, J., Ruthsatz-Stephens, K., & Ruthsatz, K. (2014). The cognitive bases of exceptional abilities in child prodigies by domain: Similarities and differences. *Intelligence, 44*(1), 11-14. https://doi.org/10.1016/j.intell.2014.01.010
5. Flavell, J. H. (1979). Metacognition and cognitive monitoring: A new area of cognitive–developmental inquiry. *American Psychologist, 34*(10), 906-911. https://doi.org/10.1037/0003-066X.34.10.906
6. Fabricius, W. V., & Schwanenflugel, P. J. (1994). The older child's theory of mind. *Advances in Psychology, 106*, 111-132. https://doi.org/10.1016/S0166-4115(08)62754-5
7. Nelson, T., & Narens, L. (1994). Why investigate metacognition? In A. Metcalfe, & P. Shimamura, *Metacognition: Knowing about knowing* (pp. 1-25). The MIT Press. https://doi.org/10.7551/mitpress/4561.001.0001
8. Efklides, A. (2001). Metacognitive experiences in problem solving: metacognition, motivation, and self-regulation. In Efklides, A., Kuhl, J., & Sorrentino, R.M. (Eds.), *Trends and prospects in motivation research*, 297-323. https://doi.org/10.1007/0-306-47676-2_16
9. Efklides, A. (2008). Metacognition: Defining its facets and levels of functioning in relation to self-regulation and co-regulation. *European Psychologist, 13*(4), 277-287. http://dx.doi.org/10.1027/1016-9040.13.4.277
10. Efklides, A. (2008). Metacognition: Defining its facets and levels of functioning in relation to self-regulation and co-regulation. *European Psychologist, 13*(4), 277-287. http://dx.doi.org/10.1027/1016-9040.13.4.277

11. Veenman, M., & Elshout, J. J. (1999). Changes in the relation between cognitive and metacognitive skills during the acquisition of expertise. *European Journal of Psychology of Education, 14,*

12. Perkins, D. N. (1985). Postprimary education has little impact on informal reasoning. *Journal of Educational Psychology, 77,* 562-570. https://doi.org/10.1037/0022-0663.77.5.562

13. Nietfeld, J. L., & Schraw, G. (2002). The effect of knowledge and strategy explanation on monitoring accuracy. *Journal of Educational Research, 95*(3), 131-142. https://doi.org/10.1080/00220670209596583

14. Bouffard-Bouchard, T. P., Parent, S., & Larivee, S. (1991). Influence of self-efficacy on self-regulation and performance among junior and senior high school age students. *International Journal of Behavioral Development, 14*(2), 153-164. http://dx.doi.org/10.1177/016502549101400203

15. Schoenfeld, A. H. (1985). *Mathematical problem solving.* New York: Academic Press.

2. The Principle Of Controlled Action

1. Heider, F. (1958). The naive analysis of action. In F. Heider, *The psychology of interpersonal relations* (pp. 79-124). John Wiley & Sons Inc. https://doi.org/10.1037/10628-004

2. Ajzen, I. (1985). From intentions to actions: A theory of planned behavior. In J. Beckmann, & J. Kuhl (Eds.), *Action control: From cognition to behavior.* Heidelberg, Berlin: Springer. https://doi.org/10.1007/978-3-642-69746-3_2

3. Ajzen, I. (1985). From intentions to actions: A theory of planned behavior. In J. Beckmann, & J. Kuhl (Eds.), *Action control: From cognition to behavior.* Heidelberg, Berlin: Springer. https://doi.org/10.1007/978-3-642-69746-3_2

4. Ajzen, I. (1985). From intentions to actions: A theory of planned behavior. In J. Beckmann, & J. Kuhl (Eds.), *Action control: From cognition to behavior.* Heidelberg, Berlin: Springer. https://doi.org/10.1007/978-3-642-69746-3_2

3. The Psychology Of Performance Improvement

1. Antony, M. M., Purdon, C. L., Huta, V., & Swinson, R. P. (1998). Dimensions of perfectionism across the anxiety disorders. *Behaviour Research and Therapy, 36*(12), 1143-115. https://doi.org/10.1016/s0005-7967(98)00083-7

2. Ferrari, J. R., Johnson, J. L., & McCown, W. G. (1995). *Procrastination and task avoidance: Theory, research and treatment.* New York: Plenum Press.

3. Stoher, J., & Joormann, J. (2001). Worry, procrastination and perfectionism: Differentiating amount of worry, pathological worry, anxiety and depression. *Cognitive Therapy and Research, 25*, 49-60. https://doi.org/10.1023/A:1026474715384

4. Tallis, F., Eysenck, M. W., & Matthews, A. (1992). A questionnaire for the measurement of nonpathological worry. *Personality and Individual Differences, 13*(2), 161-168. https://doi.org/10.1016/0191-8869(92)90038-Q

5. Efklides, A. (2002). Feelings as subjective evaluations of cognitive processing: How reliable are they? *The Journal of the Hellenic Psychological Society, 9*(2), 163-182. http://dx.doi.org/10.12681/psy_hps.24059

6. Dweck, C. S. (1989). Motivation. In Lesgold, A., & Glaser, R., (Eds.), *Foundations for a psychology of education.* Hillsdale, NJ: Erlbaum.

7. Dweck, C. S., & Leggett, E. S. (1988). A social-cognitive approach to motivation and personality. *Psychological Review, 95*(2), 256-273. https://doi.org/10.1037/0033-295X.95.2.256

8. Ames, C., & Archer, J. (1988). Achievement goals in the classroom: Students' learning strategies and motivational processes. *Journal of Applied Psychology, 80*(3), 260-267. https://doi.org/10.1037/0022-0663.80.3.260

9. Button , S. B., Mathieu, J. E., & Zajac, D. M. (1996). Goal orientation in organizational research: A conceptual and empirical foundation. *Organizational Behavior and Human Decision Processes, 67*(1), 26-48. https://doi.org/10.1006/obhd.1996.0063

10. Heyman, G. D., & Dweck, C. S. (1992). Achievement goals and intrinsic motivation: Their relation and their role in adaptive motivation. *Motivation and Emotion, 16*, 231-247. https://doi.org/10.1007/BF00991653

11. Dweck, C. S., & Leggett, E. S. (1988). A social-cognitive approach to motivation and personality. *Psychological Review, 95*(2), 256-273.

https://doi.org/10.1037/0033-295X.95.2.256

12. Elliot, A. J. (1999). Approach and avoidance motivation and achievement goals. *Educational Psychologist, 34*(3), 169-189. https://doi.org/10.1207/s15326985ep3403_3

13. Elliot, A. J., & McGregor, H. A. (2001). A 2 x 2 achievement goal framework. *Journal of Personality and Social Psychology, 80*(3), 501-519. https://doi.org/10.1037/0022-3514.80.3.501

14. Ames, C., & Archer, J. (1988). Achievement goals in the classroom: Students' learning strategies and motivational processes. *Journal of Applied Psychology, 80*(3), 260-267. https://doi.org/10.1037/0022-0663.80.3.260

15. Nolen, S. B., & Haladyna, T. M. (1990). Motivation and studying in high school science. *Journal of Research in Science and Teaching, 27*(2), 115-126. https://doi.org/10.1002/tea.3660270204

16. Schmidt, A. M., & Ford, J. K. (2006). Learning within a learner control training environment: The interactive effects of goal orientation and metacognitive instruction on learning outcomes. *Personnel Psychology, 56*(2), 405-429. https://doi.org/10.1111/j.1744-6570.2003.tb00156.x

17. Wolters, C. A., Yu, S. L., & Pintrich, P. R. (1996). The relation between goal orientation and students'motivational beliefs and self-regulated learning. *Learning and Individual Differences, 8*(3), 211-238. https://doi.org/10.1016/S1041-6080(96)90015-1

18. Butler, R. (1993). Effects of task-and ego-achievement goals on information seeking during task engagement. *Journal of Personality and Social Psychology, 65*(1), 18-31. https://doi.org/10.1037/0022-3514.65.1.18

19. Schmidt, A. M., & Ford, J. K. (2006). Learning within a learner control training environment: The interactive effects of goal orientation and metacognitive instruction on learning outcomes. *Personnel Psychology, 56*(2), 405-429. https://doi.org/10.1111/j.1744-6570.2003.tb00156.x

20. Weinstein, C., & Mayer, R. (1986). The teaching of learning strategies. In M. Wittrock (Ed.), *Handbook of research on teaching* (pp. 315-327). New York: Macmillan.

21. Elliot, A. J., McGregor, H. A., & Gable, S. (1999). Achievement goals, study strategies, and exam performance: A mediational analysis. *Journal of Educational Psychology, 91*(3), 549-563. https://doi.org/10.1037/0022-0663.91.3.549

22. Greene, B. A., & Miller, R. B. (1996). Influence on achievement: Goals, perceived ability, and cognitive engagement. *Contemporary Educational Psychology, 21*(2), 181-192. https://doi.org/10.1006/ceps.1996.0015

23. Nolen, S. B., & Haladyna, T. M. (1990). Motivation and studying in high school science. *Journal of Research in Science and Teaching, 27*(2), 115-126. https://doi.org/10.1002/tea.3660270204

24. Pintrich, P. R., & Schrauben, B. (1992). Students' motivational beliefs and their cognitive engagement in academic tasks. In D. Schunk, & J. Meece (Eds.), *Students' perception in the classroom: Causes and consequences* (pp. 149-183). Hillsdale: NJ: Erlbaum.

25. Schraw, G., Horn, C., Thorndike-Christ, T., & Bruning, R. (1995). Academic goal orientations and student classroom achievement. *Contemporary Educational Psychology, 20*(3), 359-368. https://doi.org/10.1006/ceps.1995.1023

26. Lee, O., & Anderson, C. W. (1993). Task engagement and conceptual change in middle school science classrooms. *American Education Research Journal, 30*(3), 585-610. https://doi.org/10.3102/00028312030003585

27. Nolen, S. B., & Haladyna, T. M. (1990). Motivation and studying in high school science. *Journal of Research in Science and Teaching, 27*(2), 115-126. https://doi.org/10.1002/tea.3660270204

28. Biggs, J. B. (1985). The role of metalearning in study processes. *British Journal of Educational Psychology, 55*(3), 185-212. https://doi.org/10.1111/j.2044-8279.1985.tb02625.x

29. Bouffard, T., Boisvert, J., Vezeau, C., & Larouche, C. (1995). The impact of goal orientation on self-regulation and performance among college students. *British Journal of Educational Psychology, 65*(3), 317-329. http://dx.doi.org/10.1111/j.2044-8279.1995.tb01152.x

30. Schoenfeld, A. H. (1985). *Mathematical problem solving.* New York: Academic Press.

4. Self-Efficacy: Reality Vs. Perception

1. Schwartz, H. (2002). Herbert Simon and behavioral economics. *The Journal of Socio-Economics, 31*(3), 181-189. https://doi.org/10.1016/S1053-5357(02)00161-0

2. Simon, H. A. (1959). Theories of decision-making in economics and behavioral science. *The American Economic Review, 49*(3), 253-283. http://www.jstor.org/stable/1809901

3. Bandura, A. (1977). Self-efficacy: Toward a unifying theory of behavioral change. *Psychological Review, 84*(2), 191-215. https://doi.org/10.1037/0033-295X.84.2.191

4. Bouffard-Bouchard, T. P., Parent, S., & Larivee, S. (1991). Influence of self-efficacy on self-regulation and performance among junior

and senior high school age students. *International Journal of Behavioral Development,* *14*(2), 153-164. http://dx.doi.org/10.1177/016502549101400203.

5. Bandura, A. (1993). Perceived self-efficacy in cognitive development and functioning. *Educational Psychologist, 28*(2), 117-148. https://doi.org/10.1207/s15326985ep2802_3

6. Chi, M. T., Bassok, M., Lewis, M. W., Reimann, P., & Glaser, R. (1989). Self-explanations: How students study and use examples in learning to solve problems. *Cognitive Science, 13*(2), 145-182. https://doi.org/10.1207/s15516709cog1302_1

7. Butterfield, E. C., & Nelson, G. D. (1989). Theory and practice of teaching for transfer. *ETR&D, 37,* 5-38. https://doi.org/10.1007/BF02299054

8. Dansereau, D. F. (1985). Learning strategy research. In R. Glaser, J. W. Segal, & S. F. Chipman (Eds.), *Thinking and learning skills vol. 1* (pp. 209-239). Hillsdale: Lawrence Erlbaum Associates.

9. Brown, A. L., Campione, J. C., & Day, J. D. (1981). Learning to learn: On training students to learn from texts. *Educational Researcher, 10*(2), 14-21. https://doi.org/10.3102/0013189X010002014

10. Osman, M. E., & Hannafin, M. J. (1992). Metacognition research and theory: Analysis and implications for instructional design. *Educational Technology Research and Development, 40*(2), 83-99. https://doi.org/10.1007/BF02297053

11. Osman, M. E., & Hannafin, M. J. (1992). Metacognition research and theory: Analysis and implications for instructional design. *Educational Technology Research and Development, 40*(2), 83-99. https://doi.org/10.1007/BF02297053

12. Ganz, M. N., & Ganz, B. C. (1990). Linking metacognition to classroom success. *The High School Journal, 73*(3) 180–185. http://www.jstor.org/stable/40364612

13. Reder, L. M., & Schunn, C. D. (1996). Metacognition does not imply awareness: Strategy choice is governed by implicit learning and memory. In Reder, L. M. (Ed.), *Implicit memory and metacognition.* Lawrence Erlbaum.

14. Metcalfe, J. (1994). A computationalmodeling approach to novelty monitoring, metacognition, and frontal lobe dysfunction. In J. Metcalfe , & A. P. Shimamura (Eds.), *Metacognition: Knowing about knowing* (pp. 137-156). Cambridge: MA: MIT.

5. Environmental Cultivation

1. Deci, E. L., & Ryan, R. M. (2000). The "what" and "why" of goal pursuits: Human needs and the self-determination of behavior. *Psychological Inquiry*, *11*(4), 227-268. https://doi.org/10.1207/S15327965PLI1104_01

2. Demir, M., & Özdemir, M. (2010). Friendship, need satisfaction and happiness. *Journal of Happiness Studies*, *11*, 243-259. https://doi.org/10.1007/s10902-009-9138-5

3. Tay, L., & Diener, E. (2011). Needs and subjective well-being around the world. *Journal of Personality and Social Psychology*, *101*, 354-365. https://doi.org/10.1037/a0023779

4. Diener, E., Ng, W., Harter, J., & Arora, R. (2010). Wealth and happiness across the world: Material prosperity predicts life evaluation, whereas psychosocial prosperity predicts positive feeling. *Journal of Personality and Social Psychology*, *99*(1), 52-61. https://doi.org/10.1037/a0018066

5. Baumeister, R. F., & Vohs, K. D. (2001). The pursuit of meaningfulness in life. In C. R. Snyder , & S. J. Lopez (Eds.), *Handbook of Positive Psychology* (pp. 608-618). New York: Oxford University Press.

6. Lindenberg, S. (2013). Social rationality, self-regulation and well-being: The regulatory significance of needs, goals, and the self. In R. Wittek, A. B. Snijders, & V. Nee (Eds.), *Handbook of rational choice social research* (pp. 72-112). Stanford: Stanford University Press.

7. de Waal, Frans. (2017). *The surprising science of alpha males* [Video]. TED Conferences. https://www.ted.com/talks/frans_de_waal_the_surprising_science_of_alpha_males

8. Tarayia, G. N. (2004). The legal perspectives of the Maasai culture, customs and traditions. *Arizona Journal of International & Comparative Law*, *21*(1), 183-222.

9. Deci, E. L., & Ryan, R. M. (2000). The "what" and "why" of goal pursuits: Human needs and the self-determination of behavior. *Psychological Inquiry*, *11*(4), 227-268. https://doi.org/10.1207/S15327965PLI1104_01

10. Steverink, N., Lindenberg, S., Spiegel, T., & Nieboer, A. P. (2020). The associations of different social needs with psychological strengths and subjective well-being: An empirical investigation based on Social Production Function theory. *Journal of Happiness Studies*, *21*, 799-824. https://doi.org/10.1007/s10902-019-00107-9

11. Steverink, N., Lindenberg, S., Spiegel, T., & Nieboer, A. P. (2020). The associations of different social needs with psychological

strengths and subjective well-being: An empirical investigation based on Social Production Function theory. *Journal of Happiness Studies, 21*, 799-824. https://doi.org/10.1007/s10902-019-00107-9

6. GPS (Goal Positioning System)

1. Judge, T. A., & Kammeyer-Mueller, J. D. (2012). On the value of aiming high: The causes and consequences of ambition. *Journal of Applied Psychology, 97*(4), 758-775. https://doi.org/10.1037/A0028084
2. Barsukova, O. (2016). Psychological characteristics of ambitious person. *Journal of Process Management - New Technologies, 4*(2), 79-80. http://dx.doi.org/10.5937/JPMNT1602079B
3. Jones, A. B., Sherman, R. A., & Hogan, R. T. (2017). Where is ambition in factor models of personality? *Personality and Individual Differences, 106*, 26-31. https://doi.org/10.1016/j.paid.2016.09.057
4. Huang, J., Huang, A., Ryan, K., Zabel, A., & Palmer, A. (2014). Personality and adaptive performance at work: A meta-analytic investigation. *Journal of Applied Psychology, 99*(1), 162-179. https://doi.org/10.1037/a0034285
5. Barrick, M. R., Stewart, G. L., & Piotrowski, M. (2002). Personality and job performance: Test of the mediating effects of motivation among sales representatives. *Journal of Applied Psychology, 87*(1), 43-51. https://doi.org/10.1037//0021-9010.87.1.43
6. Huang, J., Huang, A., Ryan, K., Zabel, A., & Palmer, A. (2014). Personality and adaptive performance at work: A meta-analytic investigation. *Journal of Applied Psychology, 99*(1), 162-179. https://doi.org/10.1037/a0034285

7. Identify Your Purpose

1. Hill, P. L., & Turiano, N. A. (2014). Purpose in life as a predictor of mortality across adulthood. *Psychological Science, 25*(7), 1482–1486. https://doi.org/10.1177/0956797614531799
2. Sone, T., Nakaya, N., Ohmori, K., Shimazu, T., Higashiguchi, M., Kakizaki, M., . . . Tsuji, I. (2008). Sense of life worth living (ikigai) and mortality in Japan: Ohsaki study. *Psychosomatic Medicine, 70*(6), 709-715. https://doi.org/10.1097/psy.0b013e31817e7e64
3. Freedland, K. E. (2019). The behavioral medicine research council: Its origins, mission, and methods. *Health Psychology, 38*(4), 277-289.

http://dx.doi.org/10.1037/hea0000731

4. Kim, E. S., Strecher, V. J., & Ryff, C. D. (2014). Purpose in life and use of preventive health care services. *Proceedings of the National Academy of Sciences of the United States of America, 111*(46), 16331–16336. https://doi.org/10.1073/pnas.1414826111

5. Kang, Y., Strecher, V. J., Kim, E., & Falk, E. B. (2019). Purpose in life and conflict-related neural responses during health decision-making. *Health Psychology, 38*(6), 545-552. http://dx.doi.org/10.1037/hea0000729

6. Ryan, R. M., & Deci, L. (2004). Avoiding death or engaging life as accounts of meaning and culture: comment on Pyszczynski et al. *Psychology Bulletin, 130*(3), 473-488. https://doi.org/10.1037/0033-2909.130.3.473

7. Frankl, V. E. (1985). *Man's search for meaning.* Boston: Simon and Schuster.

8. Frankl, V. E. (2014). *The will to meaning: Foundations and applications of logotherapy.* New York: NY: Plume.

9. Steger, M. F., Oishi, S., & Kashdan, T. B. (2009). Meaning in life across the life span: levels and correlates of meaning in life from emerging adulthood to older adulthood. *The Journal of, 4,* 43–52. doi:10.1080/17439760802303127

10. Baumeister, R. F., & Vohs, K. D. (2001). The pursuit of meaningfulness in life. In C. R. Snyder , & S. J. Lopez (Eds.), *Handbook of Positive Psychology* (pp. 608-618). New York: Oxford University Press.

11. Sheldon, K. M., Houser-Marko, L., & Kasser, T. (2006). Does autonomy increase with age? Comparing the goal motivations of college students and their parents. *Journal of Research in Personality, 40*(2), 168-178. https://doi.org/10.1016/j.jrp.2004.10.004

12. King, L. A. (2001). The health benefits of writing about life goals. *Personality and Social Psychology Bulletin, 27*(7), 798-807.https://doi.org/10.1177/0146167201277003

13. Higgins, R. L. (Ed.). (1990). *Self-handicapping: The paradox that isn't.* New York: Plenum. https://doi.org/10.1007/978-1-4899-0861-2

14. Jones, A. B., Sherman, R. A., & Hogan, R. T. (2017). Where is ambition in factor models of personality? *Personality and Individual Differences, 106,* 26-31. doi:https://doi.org/10.1016/j.paid.2016.09.057

15. Arkin, R. M., & Oleson, K. C. (1998). Self-handicapping. In J. M. Darley, & J. Cooper (Eds.), *Attribution processes, person perception,and social interaction: The legacy of Ned Jones.* Washington: American Psychological Association.

16. Bandura, A., & Locke, E. A. (2003). Negative self-efficacy and goal effects revisited. *Journal of Applied Psychology, 88*(1), 87-99. http://dx.doi.org/10.1037/0021-9010.88.1.87

9. Improving Your Focus

1. Csikszentmihalyi, M. (2009). Flow. In S. Lopez (Ed.), *The encyclopedia of positive psychology* (pp. 394-400). Chichester: Blackwell Publishing Ltd.
2. Csikszentmihalyi, M. (2009). Flow. In S. Lopez (Ed.), *The encyclopedia of positive psychology* (pp. 394-400). Chichester: Blackwell Publishing Ltd.
3. Stamatelopoulou, F., Pezirkianidis, C., Karakasidou, E., Lakioti, A., & Stalikas, A. (2018). "Being in the zone": A systematic review on the relationship of psychological correlates and the occurrence of flow experiences in sports' performance. *Psychology, 9*(8), 2011-2030. http://dx.doi.org/10.4236/psych.2018.98115
4. Csikszentmihalyi, M. (2009). Flow. In S. Lopez (Ed.), *The encyclopedia of positive psychology* (pp. 394-400). Chichester: Blackwell Publishing Ltd.
5. Hefferon, K., & Boniwell, I. (2011). *Positive Psychology: Theory, Research and Applications.* London: McGraw-Hill.
6. Csikszentmihalyi, M., Rathunde, K., & Whalen, S. (1993). *Talented teenagers: A longitudinal study of their development.* New York: Cambridge University Press.
7. Swann, C., Keegan, R., Piggott, D., & Crust, L. (2012). A systematic review of the experience, occurrence and controllability of flow in elite sport. *Psychology of Sport and Exercise, 13*(6), 807-819. https://doi.org/10.1016/j.psychsport.2012.05.006

Afterword

1. Clifford, C. (2017, Feb 02). Billionaire Warren Buffett discusses the book that changed his life. *CNBC.* https://www.cnbc.com/2017/02/02/billionaire-warren-buffett-discusses-the-book-that-changed-his-life.html

DISCLAIMER

The information contained in this book and its components is meant to serve as a comprehensive collection of strategies that the author of this book has done research about. Summaries, strategies, tips and tricks are only recommendations by the author, and reading this book will not guarantee that one's results will exactly mirror the author's results.

The author of this book has made all reasonable efforts to provide current and accurate information for the readers of this book. The author and their associates will not be held liable for any unintentional errors or omissions that may be found.

The material in the book may include information by third parties. Third party materials are comprised of opinions expressed by their owners. As such, the author of this book does not assume responsibility or liability for any third party material or opinions.

Manufactured by Amazon.ca
Acheson, AB